SPECIAL NEEDS IN ORDINAR)
General editor: Peter Mittler
Associate editors: Mel Ainscow,
Rosemary Webb and Sheila Wolfe......

C000133047

Opening Doors

Titles in the Special Needs in Ordinary Schools series

Opening Doors

Learning Support
in Higher Education

Edited by Sheila Wolfendale
and Jenny Corbett

CASSELL

Cassell

Wellington House
125 Strand
London WC2R 0BB

127 West 24th Street
New York
NY 10011

First published 1996

British Library Cataloguing-in-Publication Data
A catalogue record for this book is available from the British Library.

ISBN 0-304-33508-8 (hardback)
ISBN 0-304-33509-6 (paperback)

Typeset by Action Typesetting, Northgate Street, Gloucester
Printed and Bound in Great Britain by Biddles Limited, Guildford and King's Lynn

Contents

Editorial foreword

This book is about access and entitlement to higher education. Its starting point is the need for institutions of higher education to respond more fully and more imaginatively to the rich diversity of a student population which bears little resemblance to that of a generation ago. Many of today's HE students bring a wealth of practical experience and knowledge, even though they may lack traditional academic qualifications. Many are part-time and are coping with the demands of work and with family responsibilites. An increasing number come from communites where young people in the past left school with little or no prospects of further opportunities for study. To them, higher education is not the natural culmination of GCSE and A-level studies at 18 but a long struggle founded on a passionate commitment to lifelong learning.

Included in the new generation of HE students are those whose experience was one of failure and frustration and who left school with little or nothing to show by way of paper qualifications – casualties of the system in their time. Some will already have experienced a 'career' and perhaps a label associated with one or more of the categories of special educational need. A small minority will have passed through special schools because of significant physical or sensory impairments. They will continue to require individually tailored support systems at university. A rapidly growing number will have specific learning difficulties/dyslexia which continue to have an adverse effect on their ability to benefit from HE. But an increasing majority will be products (sometimes survivors) of the evolving systems of special needs provision in ordinary schools who would not in previous generations have been able to study to HE level. It is hardly surprising that many of the new generation of students have a right to high quality support in acquiring and strengthening study skills and that this should be standard rather than special provision in all universities and colleges. The new universities have a much better track record in providing such support.

It is clear that all students need not only access to building (by means of ramps and other alterations to the built environment) but a reappraisal of the curriculum and the modes of its delivery, and a commitment to ensure access to the whole range of learning and social experiences open to other students.

It follows that an increasing proportion of today's students will at some time, or during the whole of their sudies, require 'provision beyond that which is generally available'. This book is about the nature of such support systems. It is also about the organizational, management and systemic changes which the HE sector as a whole will need to make to respond more fully in the future to the needs of the new generation of students.

Readers will readily detect many parallels between changes in schools and in universities. What started as a demand for access for students with physical and sensory impairments is now nothing less than a recognition of the need for a reorganization and restructuring of planning and provision for all students. This in turn calls for a reappraisal of management practices which reflect discriminatory attitudes and assumptions. There are parallels also in the requirement to produce clear policy statements and to ensure that students receive the technical and personal support which they need.

The response of the HE sector to such student diversity has been characteristically mixed. Some institutions are light years ahead of others in changing their provision and in providing flexible support. They have long enjoyed a good reputation for meeting the needs of disabled students. Others have taken advantage of pump priming by the HE Funding Councils to set up sustainable and high quality support systems. The contributors to this book celebrate examples of good practice while also highlighting the major obstacles which have been encountered even in the most forward looking institutions.

I hope that this book will be studied in depth and detail by all committees and individuals with responsibility for ensuring access to higher education and for improving the quality of learning experiences for all students.

Peter Mittler
University of Manchester
June 1996

Contributors

Deborah Cooper is the Director of Skill: National Bureau for Students with Disabilities. She previously worked as a teacher and community worker with a range of people with disabilities and learning difficulties. She has written a number of articles and books.

Jenny Corbett is a Senior Lecturer at the Institute of Education, London. Before teaching in HE, she taught in mainstream and special schools and in a college of further education, where she was a Learning Support Co-ordinator. Her long-term research interest is in post-compulsory education for students with physical and learning disabilities. She has published widely in the areas of special needs and further education.

Sophie Corlett is Assistant Director of Skill, where she has responsibility for higher education issues. She has previously worked both for another disability organization and in Parliament.

Stella ni Ghallchoir Cottrell taught history at Somerville College, Oxford, for four years. She trained as a teacher in English and communications, and has been involved in community projects, including helping to develop and teach Return to Learn and Second Chance to Learn schemes (WEA, Oxford). She taught at Hackney College in London before her appointment at the University of East London in 1990 as Senior Lecturer in Learning Development (Study Skills). She has developed the Dyslexia Service at UEL since 1991 and been Dyslexia Consultant to several universities and colleges.

Alan Hurst works in the Department of Education Studies at the University of Central Lancashire and is also an Adviser for Disabled Students. Currently he is Senior Vice-Chair of Skill and convenes both the national Higher Education Working party and the North West regional HE group. He is a member of the HEFC Advisory Group on Access and Widening Participation and of its Disability Subgroup. His research interests and publications are in the area of HE and disability. He has lectured widely in many European countries.

Peter McDonald was born in Jamaica in 1965. He has cerebral palsy. After coming to England in 1971, he spent ten years in special education and then attended a mainstream college. He spent four years at university, gaining a degree in sociological research in 1990. He worked as a researcher for Scope (formerly the Spastics Society) before becoming a freelance researcher and writer.

Jean McGinty was a former member of HMI with responsibility for students in further and higher education with learning difficulties and disabilities. Currently, she is Vice-president of Skill, member of the Prince of Wales Advisory Group on Disability and chairperson of the National Organisation for Adult Learning (NIACE), Learning Difficulties and/or Disabilities Education Policy Committee. She is co-author of *Learning Support for Young People in Transition* and *Further Education in the Market Place* (both with John Fish).

Lea Myers is a researcher and lecturer in education at the Education and Community Studies Department, University of East London.

Viv Parker is a Senior Lecturer in Education and University Co-ordinator for Students with Disabilities and Special Needs at the Education and Community Studies Department, University of East London.

Robert Simpson is a Senior Lecturer at the University of East London where he works in the Learning Development Unit which has responsibility for promoting learning development entitlement across the university. Previously, he has worked abroad and in secondary, adult, further and higher education in the UK.

Tony Wailey is an AP(E)L (Assessment of Prior Experience and Learning) and Mature Student Adviser at the Centre for Access, Advice and Continuing Education at the University of East London. Previously, he has worked in guidance centres and adult, further and higher education. He has published in many fields, particularly in relation to mature students and their learning demands.

Jenni Wallace is the Educational Development Co-ordinator at the Surrey Institute of Art and Design, having left Kingston University to pursue her research into the ways of learning in an art and design context. She has worked previously at London University Institute of Education and also extensively in special education, social services and mental health. She has led the Supplemental Instruction Project in the UK since 1990 liaising with American colleagues. She is also a visiting academic at the Universities of Natal and Witwatersrand, South Africa.

Sheila Wolfendale has been a primary school and remedial reading teacher, an educational psychologist in several LEAs and is currently Director of the MSc and Doctorate in Educational Psychology training programme at the University of East London. She has written and edited many books, chapters, articles and handbooks on aspects of special needs, early years and parental involvement. She was recently awarded a PhD by published works.

Learning support in higher education: principles, values, continuities

Sheila Wolfendale

DEFINING LEARNING SUPPORT IN HE

This chapter sets the scene for the book as a whole and provides a context for the contributions. As the writing of the book progressed it became clearer to both editors that the conception of 'Learning Support' was broad and encompassing: it embraces meeting the needs of those students who request and perhaps require targeted extra, or additional help to progress in their studies; it refers to a general, underlying principle, increasingly current in higher education, that students are entitled to be considered as learners, not merely as disciples and future exponents of a specialist subject discipline. This latter conception acknowledges that university is not just an apprenticeship stage but a period of learning in its own right. This view is consistent with a view of 'lifelong learning' (see p. 14).

Learning Support in higher education, therefore, reflects and embodies an inclusive ideology, within a stage of education paradoxically, which has long been associated with selection and élitism. Indeed, higher education is characterized in part by its rigid selection criteria which filters out the eligible few from the ineligible many. Learning Support recognizes and acknowledges that students have differential learning needs, study at different rates and paces, and manifest a myriad of learning styles. Such an ideology does not have to compromise traditional conceptions of subject or discipline learning. Rather, it promotes and enhances the idea of striving to achieve excellence. Adherents of a broader conception of Learning Support are mindful of the periodic moral panic expressed in the media by 'traditionalists': the alleged falling standards in A-level results and the consequent lowering of degree standards, allied to an alleged lowering of the academic achievement and even ability of the HE student intake. Such an entrenched view (Daley, 1995) flies in the face of realities to which the present government has avowedly been committed, namely, expansion of HE and a more flexible view of entry criteria that truly opens up HE to many who missed opportunities earlier on in their lives.

GENESIS AND RATIONALE OF THE BOOK

In HE this decade has become significant within the area of Learning Support generally and special needs and disability in particular. Provision has expanded and staff expertise is manifestly growing in areas of enhancing student learning, assessment and intervention. In many instances, these developments, often innovative, have been supported by government funding. Two examples are the Enterprise in Higher Education (see below) and the two-year initiative funded by HEFCE described in this book by Alan Hurst (Chapter 9), Deborah Cooper and Sophie Corlett (Chapter 10) and discussed by Viv Parker and Lea Myers in Chapter 5, and Jenny Corbett and Jean McGinty in Chapter 6.

It seemed to the editors that much of this work needed to be reported and celebrated within a publication that could inspire future applications elsewhere. Most of the chapters describe work in the sphere of special needs and disability and this reflects the fact that this is presently an area of significant innovation. Stella ni Gallchoir Cottrell (Chapter 4) provides an account of provision for students with specific learning difficulties (dyslexia) at the University of East London (UEL) and Peter McDonald (Chapter 8) gives a graphic personal account from the perspective of being disabled within the school, further and higher education systems. In keeping with the inclusive philosophy of this book, three chapters in particular take the broadest view of ways of supporting learning. These are by Robert Simpson (Chapter 2), Tony Wailey (Chapter 3), and Jenni Wallace (Chapter 7). Jenny Corbett's concluding chapter relates developments in the UK to a number of policy and practice approaches in other countries.

The rest of this introductory chapter will identify and highlight a number of principles and themes, several of which are further described, illustrated and discussed in later chapters. We hope that the book itself will convey the message that Learning Support provision in higher education is one positive response to the challenges facing the HE providers and all those charged with responsibilities to plan and implement quality education in the UK for the new millennium.

PRINCIPLES AND VALUES UNDERLYING LEARNING SUPPORT IN HE

Within a broad definition of Learning Support, such as that offered above, there are a number of embedded, core principles, which constitute the ideological engine, so to speak, that drives Learning Support in practice: entitlement, students' rights, equal opportunities, access, inclusion, and continuity.

Apart from what should be a bedrock principle of any student's human right to be treated with respect and as a partner in the learning enterprise, students have a fundamental right to be respected as learners. A number of universities affirm this as a basic right in their policy statements on equal opportunities. This tenet is expressed in the following extract from the UEL Faculty of Science and Health Learning Support Policy:

> All learners are entitled to a range of learning opportunities which will enable them to fulfil their learning goals and improve their life chances. Some learners will require specific additional support in order to help them meet these goals and to allow them to participate and achieve fully. Students are entitled to expect and be guaranteed a sympathetic and constructive response to requests for support. (Wolfendale, 1994a, p.1)

Learning Support is by definition an inclusive approach, since it applies to all students within a given HE institution. However, I suggest that 'inclusion' carries with it additional meaning, related to and derived from concepts of integration and inclusion at school level.

We have witnessed during the past ten to twenty years a progressive movement towards the educational integration of pupils with special educational needs and disabilities, and supporting literature on these developments is fast accumulating (Fulcher, 1989; Slee, 1993). A spirit of inclusion has permeated higher education manifested by practices that seek to meet the learning and other needs of students with 'special needs'. For example, provision for students with physical disability, or hearing or visual impairment is designed to support their learning alongside their student colleagues and friends, thus reducing or eliminating the risks of marginalizing such students. This is a manifestation of continuity between the successive stages of education, a theme which is explored further below.

ENHANCING AND VALUING THE STUDENT LEARNING EXPERIENCE

Robert Simpson in Chapter 2 outlines the notion of learning entitlement and Tony Wailey in Chapter 3, describes how a wider interpretation of the function of AP(E)L can be used to integrate guidance and learning development in the academic context, and formally incorporates and values prior learning, experience and qualifications. They therefore present a conception of 'learning' that goes beyond a narrow view of student learning being related exclusively to the degree subject(s), towards one that acknowledges that learning occurs and accrues continuously.

David Gosling (1995) points out that nowadays there are greater pressures upon student learners. Some of these are associated with the increase in learning technology and the increasing requirement to build into teaching/learning the acquisition of personal and transferable skills. Gosling perceives the need for an integrated learning approach which will assist students to achieve these objectives:

- the enhancement of appropriate language skills, familiarization with systematic techniques of information gathering, recording and presentation, and higher level skills of critical thinking, reasoning and problem solving
- an introduction to the application of information technology
- the development of personal and transferable skills, such as the ability to work in groups, listen to and respond to others; to manage time effectively, and to be able to carry out self-appraisal, goal-setting and task management
- to encourage students to become more aware of their learning style and learning needs and to develop effective ways of studying and learning

The five-year (starting 1987, with different HE institutions subsequently entering at different times) government-backed Enterprise in Higher Education (EHE) initiative promoted as a key objective the development of a range of student-centred learning mechanisms within and across the many participating institutions. Such mechanisms have included piloting Records of Achievement and Profiling (Fenwick, Assiter and Nixon, 1992; Halsall *et al.*, 1995), Learning Contracts (Paul and Shaw, 1991), and fostering core/personal transferable skills, such as those cited above by Gosling.

These teaching/learning innovations are increasingly becoming a standard part of course life (as can be attested, first-hand, on the UEL MSc Educational Psychology course; see Wolfendale, 1994b), and are fulfilling the aims and goals of the EHE initiative which was designed overall to:

- bridge the perceived HE/world of work gap
- address employers' expressed criticisms that graduates are often insufficiently equipped with a range of requisite reasoning and communication skills
- maximize the teaching/learning experience for providers and recipients (Department of Employment Group, 1991).

A second-year EHE project evaluation (NFER, 1991, p.4) reported that 'in general, the EHE initiative appeared to have made a successful start towards achieving its objectives'. A CNAA report (1992) provides a number of case studies in student-centred learning which, collectively, constitute a positive affirmation of this recent phenomenon, which, the report notes, is one concept within 'a family of concepts which describe a flexible approach to learning sometimes grouped ... other members of the family include *distance learning, independent learning*' (CNAA, 1992, p.1). See also equivalent terms 'learner-managed learning' and 'self-directed learning' (Hammond and Collins, 1991), and 'co-operative learning' (Johnson and Johnson, 1987; Topping, 1992), 'peer tutoring' (Goodlad and Hirst, 1990; Topping, 1995) and Jenni Wallace's Chapter 7 in this book.

Explicit in a number of these initiatives is the notion that, as new mechanisms are being introduced to support learning, so these also call for reappraisal of teaching, and traditional 'chalk and talk' set-piece lectures give way to participant seminars. Even in those instances where set-piece lectures to huge numbers of students are unavoidable, increasingly lecturers adopt technological aids (from overhead projectors and slides to closed-circuit television and video, including interactive video) to deliver their lectures in ways which facilitate student learning.

A rather more rigorous approach than has customarily obtained to appraising teaching standards in higher education is advocated in a Green Paper from the Committee of Vice-Chancellors and Principals (CVCP, 1991). It proposes the establishment of a set of appropriate criteria by which quality and excellence in teaching in higher education can be identified. The proposals expressed in this publication would elevate the status of teaching in higher education and, if adopted, would ensure that teaching excellence becomes an integral part of 'Total Quality Management'; see also a later CVCP Green Paper (unnumbered, by Entwhistle, 1992) for a comprehensive literature review on the impact of teaching on learning outcomes in higher education.

SPECIAL NEEDS IN HIGHER EDUCATION

A central stance of this book is that Learning Support in higher education is broad and encompassing; it can be conceptualized along a continuum, at one end of which are those students with specific, 'special' needs. Pro-inclusive educationalists (see earlier references; also Clark *et al.*, 1995) found the continuum idea one which perpetuates a special needs/mainstream dichotomy, and continues to marginalize 'special' needs from the rest of a given population. An alternative conception is that all students have distinctive, differential 'learning needs' to which higher education providers should have 'due regard'. In this view, Learning Support is less a continuum than it is a systemic framework which can be absorbed integrally within the overall provision of an higher education institution. It is hoped that the chapters in this book describing special needs provision at UEL convey a picture of provision initiated as much at a systemic, organizational level as within different faculties and at individual course level.

Terminology and the 'language' of 'special needs' (Corbett, 1994; 1996) is as important in higher education as it is at school and within further education. For example, a working party set up to develop a policy on Learning Support, within the Faculty of Science and Health at UEL, chaired by this author, considered and grappled with definitions. The final Policy Statement (Wolfendale, 1994a) poses the question '*Who is the policy for?*' and states that it is:

> for students whose progress at UEL and within the faculty might be hindered by: specific learning difficulties (dyslexia); language/communication difficulties; needing advice and support with study skills; a physical/sensory disability. If a student (and his/her tutors) are concerned that these are 'problems' impeding progress, then this policy applies. (p. 1)

It is acknowledged, within this definition, that perception is paramount, and that the student's own view, as well as that of tutors, is the major determinant in the initial identification of a 'special', or distinctive learning need; (see the discussion of terminology in Chapter 5 given by Myers and Parker.

Chapter 9 by Alan Hurst and Chapter 10 by Deborah Cooper and Sophie Corlett trace and describe the progressive recognition and acknowledgement of distinctive learning needs in higher education, especially as they relate to identified 'special needs' in respect of students with disabilities. The next section explores and highlights a number of related issues.

Transition and continuities

Higher education has not remained immune and isolated from the rest of the education system in respect of special needs. Indeed, the 1978 Warnock Report (also referred to by Cooper and Corlett in Chapter 10) includes a page on HE and makes mention of those few HE institutions at the time (1970s) which made provision for deaf and/or physically handicapped students. Warnock's major recommendation echoes to this day:

> We recommend that all universities ... as well as other establishments of higher education should formulate and publicise a policy on the admission of students with disabilities or significant difficulties and should make systematic arrangements to meet the welfare and special needs, including careers counselling, of those who are admitted. (para. 10.49, p. 177)

This recommendation resonates today because it is not the case that each and every higher education institution does have such a written policy, let alone inclusive provision for students with disabilities.

The Warnock model promotes the notion of continuity throughout all phases of education, recognizing, in the spirit of *entitlement*, referred to above, that some students will continue to have specific support needs. Educational legislation, in the area of special educational needs and focusing upon school levels has been comprehensive (1981 Education Act, replaced by the 1993 Education Act, Part 3) and, since 1994, and as part of the 1993 Education Act, special educational needs assessment and provision are governed and guided by the Code of Practice (HMSO, 1994). Continuity into post-school provision is enhanced by reference, in the Code of Practice, to the Transition Plan, linking school and post-school, especially further education provision for special needs. Reciprocally, inclusion of the Transition Plan and the explicit FE link reflects the significant burgeoning of FE special needs provision of the last few years – and indeed builds upon reference to FE in the Warnock Report (Corbett, 1990; McGinty and Fish, 1992; Sutcliffe, 1992), and recent government circulars (FEFC, 1994; 1995) on 'Students with Learning Difficulties and/or Disabilities'. These circulars set out arrangements and guidance for students in FE colleges and specialist colleges outside the FE sector.

David Johnstone's book (1995) in the series *Special Needs in the Ordinary School* of which this book is a part, provides a comprehensive review of such provision and concomitant issues, and reinforces school – further education – higher education continuity, particularly in his final chapter, 'Emerging issues and future directions across the spectrum of further and higher education'. He refers to widening participation in higher education, with the commensurate increase of numbers of students with disabilities, but points out that representation is still disproportionate. 'This issue of disproportionate representation in HE circles has long been shared by disabled people with other marginalised groups in society' (p.175). Likewise, he avers, provision for disabled students in higher education is still inadequate. Barriers which operate as obstacles to widening participation include market and policy limitations, physical environment, student support (costs of HE) and funding, i.e. the need for extra, targeted funding to meet special needs.

While acknowledging that the HEFCE Special Initiatives project and the Disabled Students' Allowance – see Hurst (Chapter 9) and Cooper and Corlett (Chapter 10) – have undoubtedly made a difference, Johnstone's view is that it is still not enough. Provision should be extended (the HEFCE initiative was intended to be a pump primer and stimulate future developments), attitudes and expectations should change:

> If HE is to be offered as an attractive and acceptable alternative in the post-school sector, more attention needs to be paid to the provision of equipment that is effective and more recognition given to the autonomous voice of people who are seeking to break the chain of dependence through access to HE. (p. 178)

Johnstone's final strictures accord with the theme of continuity of provision, espoused in this chapter, that 'up to now the development of school-college links has been encouraged and promoted … now HE must join in too' (p. 179).

In Chapter 8, Peter MacDonald powerfully charts a number of these continuity/discontinuity issues through the lens of one 'consumer' of educational services who has experienced all the phases.

Expanding 'special' provision: meeting the need?

As we have seen, there is accumulating evidence that special needs and disability issues are on the higher education agenda, but we cannot yet forecast whether or not

- the pace of change and innovation will be sustained, once the effects of the HEFCE 'special initiatives' financial boost have ceased
- some special needs areas will be perceived to be priority areas to

be protected and maintained, as against others which will 'wither on the vine' once the special initiatives money has been withdrawn

- all institutions of higher education will adopt a written policy commitment to special needs and disability, as urged in the Warnock Report
- 'special needs' issues will become subsumed within an institution's Learning Support strategy and become embedded within equal opportunities and student rights, and consequently, part of that institution's culture.

These four points are addressed below.

Effects of the HEFCE 'special initiatives'

Deborah Cooper and Sophie Corlett (in Chapter 10) cogently describe the varied and differential responses of HE institutions to this opportunity. Pointing out that the HE special needs/disability 'landscape' has significantly altered in the last ten years, they also aver, somewhat gloomily, that some of the initiatives will not sustain once the HEFCE grant ceases. Yet innovation was ever thus: the pace of change and the adoption of a universally agreed agenda is rarely smoothly linear and sequential; conversion and commitment proceed in a series of bumps and lurches – individuals and institutions need time to conceptually absorb, challenge existing assumptions and embedded attitudes, learn from others, introduce and evaluate.

Inspiration and encouragement can be drawn from the various interim reports on the HEFCE 'Special Initiatives', which, we must remind ourselves, was government money set aside 'to encourage widening participation for students with special needs'. These reports (e.g. HEFCE, 1995; Skill, 1995) describe how each institution in receipt of the funds has responded. A mapping analysis of institutional initiatives (Wolfendale, reproduced in Skill, 1995, p. 7) for the 1993–94 cohort identifies most and least areas of special need/disability under development within the participating institutions. Skill has repeated the exercise for 1994–95 (Skill, 1995).

Areas of most take-up during 1993–95 included Specific Learning Difficulties (dyslexia), provision for sensory impairment (hearing, vision) and physical disability, and areas of least development include more structural and policy aspects such as admissions procedures, environmental adaptation and staff development. In 1994–95, under three categories added by Skill to Wolfendale's original ten categories (which had reflected initiative areas during 1993–94) we find initiatives focusing on general learning/learner support, access arrangements and information technology (IT).

Analogies with the school and further education systems can again be made. As special needs/disability have become higher profile, with commensurate advances in provision in schools and colleges, so have staff expertise and knowledge become increasingly sophisticated. In higher education, we can predict that theory and methodology will develop hand in hand with advances in provision, more speedily in some areas than in others. The following discussion further illuminates this point.

Differential effects: varying priorities

Some of these identified areas are gaining momentum in terms of provision and growing staff expertise; others may be vulnerable as Cooper and Corlett point out in Chapter 10. Areas such as physical, hearing and visual disability depend crucially upon capital investment in environmental adaptation and supporting technology, including IT. However, as again mentioned by Cooper and Corlett, other areas are perceived to be 'growth areas', e.g. specific learning difficulties (dyslexia), as the mapping analysis referred to above attests. This area warrants some discussion – issues of definition and labelling remain contentious right through the phases of the education system (Pumfrey and Reason, 1991 and Chapter 4 by Stella Cottrell). Ignorance and misunderstanding of the 'syndrome' remain widespread, as a survey of attitudes to and understanding of 'dyslexia' at UEL (at that time, the Polytechnic of East London) confirmed (Wolfendale, 1992).

However, research and knowledge have proceeded apace, and the HEFCE National Working Party on Dyslexia in Higher Education, alluded to by Cooper and Corlett, epitomizes an attempt to draw together the issues and to make recommendations. There is considerable expertise within this working party; it comprises thirteen members and is chaired by Dr Chris Singleton, Psychology Department, University of Hull. The nine specific objectives of the working party include: carrying out a survey of existing provision, consulting with HE institutions, reviewing existing test and assessment procedures, considering and formulating a variety of models. The working party is due to report during the autumn of 1996.

Thus the area of Specific Learning Difficulties (dyslexia) provides a singular and distinctive example of 'most' development to date. Vigilance is required to ensure that all identified special needs and disability areas are not put at risk. Under equal opportunities it would be invidious if some areas were regarded and treated as more 'important' than others.

This brings me to the final two points – policy and commitment.

Policy and commitment

The formulation of Learning Support, defined and adopted in this book embraces the learning needs of all students as has already been discussed, and subsumes a whole range of minor/temporary needs to more enduring identified 'special' needs. Equal opportunities policies beg the question as to whether or not institutions can really meet all such identified needs. Such a commitment means recognizing and responding to the nature of learning support need even when some aspects of 'need' have not traditionally been acknowledged as such, for example, *study skills*.

The author, with a colleague Chris Thornton (now Head of Student Services at Brighton University) ran and evaluated a pilot Study Skills Drop-In facility over the period of one academic year (Wolfendale, 1992). Among other findings, we confirmed a range of minor to more significant study skill problems. From this a continuum model (Table 1.1) was postulated (Wolfendale, 1992, p. 7).

Evidently there are students who enter higher education with residual literacy needs, and/or with an inappropriate and underdeveloped repertoire of study skills. This must always have been the case and perhaps some readers will relate to these comments from their own and peer experience. The point is whether, within a policy of Learning Support, higher education institutions now recognize that this area can be problematic, and that they can and should be pro-active in terms of providing the necessary support.

A commitment to meeting students' needs as expressed in any policy has to encompass all areas and all degrees of severity of need. At this time, as the mapping analysis described above confirms, only a minority of higher education institutions addressed themselves to issues of principles and policy during the two-year HEFCE 'Special Initiatives' (six in 1993–94 and four in 1994–95). As an example of good practice, Alan Hurst (Chapter 9) describes developments at Sheffield Hallam University. Initiatives there are built upon a clear conceptualization and seven key principles.

Comments in the final part of this chapter relate some of the developments described to overall issues of quality assurance.

Table 1.1: *A continuum model of study problems (Wolfendale, 1992)*

COMMONLY REPORTED BY MOST STUDENTS	⟷	REPORTED BY SIGNIFICANT MINORITY	⟷	REPORTED BY SMALL MINORITY OF STUDENTS
• work motivation • work organization • exam anxiety (often 'psychological' problems, not always backed up by 'evidence')		• spelling difficulties+ • note-taking difficulties • reading for information and meaning difficulties • essay writing/expression difficulties + + (can be backed up by evidence from assessment and inspection of written work)		Problems as cited on left ⟶ but appear consistently, are persistent and unimprovable without structured, sustained intervention. (confirmed by evidence and from tutors)

COMMENTS

Several students reported these anxieties; it is noted that (a) they were finalists (b) exit data, July 1990, shows they each received either 2:1 or 2:2 degree passes. The Drop In operates without external referral criteria. These students had every right to self-refer for perceived problems that are nowhere near as severe as those on the right of the continuum.	These cited problems are within so-called normal range of competence at the higher-order literacy skills. They are often not seen as particularly severe by students or staff, who may correct error in written work. Collectively these difficulties may form a syndrome and thus warrant concern; individually they may not impede progress towards a degree even if they do reduce performance.	The criteria for concern and justifying action (referral, help) are as cited above. Individually and collectively the 'symptoms' are severe and students have never attained functional competence within the repertoire of higher-order literacy skills. These students may be considered to have 'special needs' that should be met by extra support and resources.

ASSURING QUALITY IN LEARNING SUPPORT

This book, as a whole, seeks to reflect contemporary views concerning the inclusive nature of Learning Support. We have seen that advocates of this position recognize a number of bedrock core principles and values. They also acknowledge that there are certain current realities and imperatives that drive such an inclusive approach.

One is the current emphasis upon quality assurance mechanisms in higher education. Predicated upon 'value for money' considerations, institutions are urged by government to have in place a range of 'performance indicators' which can be used to assess the 'service delivery' of the provider institutions and which, being accessible and in the public domain, constitute an unprecedented form of accountability. These mechanisms, now mandatory, apply throughout the education system; at school level they appear in the form of Ofsted (Office for Standards in Education) indicators of school effectiveness and in published school 'league tables' of examination results.

Quality assurance procedures at UEL provide a case in point and echo those procedures currently under development at other higher education establishments. The UEL initiated its QILT drive (Quality Improvement in Teaching and Learning) during 1993–94. The principles and practice which are outlined in a number of publications (HEQC, 1994; UEL 1995a; UEL, 1995b) permeate all areas of university life. One of the most recent publications is a booklet for students (UEL, 1995c) which outlines eight ways in which students can become involved with mechanisms towards the *'assurance and assessment of quality within the university'*. The student booklet declares

> We recognise that students make a valuable contribution to the assurance and assessment of quality ... we are therefore committed to seeking the views of all our students about their course of study and their learning environment and to use what they tell us to improve the quality of their educational experience. (p. 1)

Such quality assurance methodology aims to enshrine and embed learning support integrally within all university provision. As far as special needs and disability are concerned, macro-level institutional response will, in future, have to have due regard to the requirements of the Disability Discrimination Act 1995 – another imperative. As Cooper and Corlett describe in Chapter 10, all higher education establishments will have to produce regular 'disability statements' on how they meet the needs of disabled students. While there is a view that this requirement does not go far enough in laying down obligations in this area, nevertheless there will be a greater degree of transparency and accountability in what institutions do provide beneath the overall umbrella of Learning Support, which will surely, gradually, lead to improvements.

A final referent, of global dimensions, is the conception of lifelong learning. At the end of 1995, the UK government produced a draft document *Lifetime Learning: Consultation Document* (not referenced, since it will be superseded, during 1996, by the final version), which accepted two fundamental premises: that we continue to be learners all our lives and that there should be continuing lifelong opportunities to learn in a formal sense (e.g. attendance on courses, including award-bearing courses) as well as informal and incidental ways. At the same time, the European Commission launched a paper on lifelong learning, to presage 1996 as the European Year of Lifelong Learning (European Commission, 1995). A pervasive theme of this paper is that society must invest in intelligence and learning. In the UK, a national Campaign for Learning was launched during the autumn of 1995 (Royal Society of Arts, 1995). Its main aim is to help create a 'learning society' within which lifelong learning is integral.

The intention behind these initiatives is both humanitarian and economic. In the same spirit, higher education institutions are increasingly committed to providing learning opportunities and learning support to all students within their communities. We will enter the new millennium with an altered conception of higher education, one which acknowledges and seeks to foster and support the latent talent of its students, without compromising quality in learning and teaching.

Initiatives referred to in this and other chapters may be seen as the ultimate test of an inclusive educational philosophy. This chapter began with a recognition that higher education has traditionally been élitist and selective. There is a prevalent resistance to changing this characteristic by altering the nature of the learning community. A possible scenario is the covert establishment of higher education streaming to cater for different needs. As with any commitment to an inclusive policy, it would be unwise to ignore the potential for conflict. Traditionalists will continue to be arraigned against those who believe that there is evidence that collective academic standards are not jeopardized by these 'new' opportunities or by a declared institutional commitment to learning support for all in higher education.

REFERENCES

Clark, C., Dyson, A. and Millward, A. (eds) (1995) *Towards inclusive schools?* London: David Fulton.

CNNA (1992) *Case Studies in Student-centred Learning,* Project report 36. London: CNAA.

CVCP (1991) Committee of Vice-Chancellors and Principals Occasional Green Paper, No. 1 *Teaching Standards and Excellence in Higher Education: Developing a Culture for Quality.* Sheffield: CVCP.

Corbett, J. (ed.) (1990) *Uneasy Transitions, Disaffection in Post-Compulsory Education and Training.* London: Falmer.

Corbett, J. (1994) Special language and political correctness, *British Journal of Special Education,* **21** (1), 17–19.

Corbett, J. (1996) *Badmouthing: the Language of Special Needs.* London: Falmer.

Daley, J. (1995) The fall in A-level subjects, *The Times,* 17 August.

Department of Employment Group (1991) *Enterprise in Higher Education: Key Features 1990–91.* Sheffield: The Group.

Disability Discrimination Act (1995), *Disability on the Agenda: Brief Guide.* London: HMSO.

Entwhistle, N. (1992) *The Impact of Teaching on Learning Outcomes in Higher Education: A Literature Review.* Sheffield: Committee of Vice-Chancellors and Principals.

European Commission (1995) *Teaching and Learning: Towards a Knowledge-based Society.* Brussels: EC.

FEFC (1994) *Circular 94/03 Students with learning difficulties and/or disabilities,* 28 February. Coventry: FEFC.

FEFC (1995) *Circular 95/07 Students with learning difficulties and/or disabilities* 17 February. Coventry: FEFC.

Fenwick, A., Assiter, A., and Nixon, N. (1992) *Profiling in Higher Education.* Sheffield: Department of Employment Group.

Fulcher, G. (1989) *Disabling Policies? A Comparative Approach to Education Policy and Disability.* Lewes: Falmer.

Goodlad, S. and Hirst, B. (eds) (1990) *Explorations in Peer Tutoring.* Englewood Cliffs: Prentice-Hall.

Gosling, D. (1995) *On Course: Academic Guidance and Learning Development.* London: Educational Development Services, University of East London.

Halsall, R., Hustler, D., Carter, K. and Green, J. (1995) Recording achievement and higher education, *Journal of Further and Higher Education,* **19, (2),** 30–40.

Hammond, M. and Collins, P. (1991) *Self-directed Learning.* London: Kogan-Page.

HEFCE (1995) *Access to HE: Students with Special Needs* – HEFCE Report on the 1993–1994 Special Initiative to Encourage Widening Participation for Students with Special Needs). Bristol: HEFCE.

HEQC Higher Education Quality Council (1994), *UEL Quality Audit Report.* Birmingham: Quality Assurance Group.

HMSO (1994) *Code of Practice on the Identification and Assessment of Special Educational Needs*. London: HMSO.

Johnson, D. and Johnson, R. (1987) *Learning Together and Alone*. (2nd edn). Englewood Cliffs: Prentice-Hall.

Johnstone, D. (1995) *Further Opportunities: Learning Difficulties and Disabilities in Further Education*. London: Cassell.

McGinty, J. and Fish, J. (1992) *Learning Support for Young People in Transition*. Buckingham: Open University Press.

NFER National Foundation for Educational Research (1991) *Enterprise in Higher Education (EHE) Initiative* (Second Year National Evaluation Summary Report). Slough: NFER.

Paul, V. and Shaw, M. (1991) *A Manual of Contract Learning*. Leeds: Leeds Polytechnic.

Pumfrey, P. and Reason, R. (eds) (1991) *Specific Learning Difficulties (Dyslexia): Challenges and Responses*. London: Routledge.

Skill (1995) *Projects Update*. London: Skill.

Slee, R. (ed.) (1993) *Is There a Desk With My Name on it? The Politics of Integration*. Lewes: Falmer.

Sutcliffe, J. (1992) *Integration for Adults with Learning Difficulties*. Leicester: National Institute of Adult Continuing Education.

Topping, K. (1992) Cooperative learning and peer tutoring; an overview. *Psychologist*, **5**, 151–7.

Topping, K. (1995) Organising peer tutoring in higher and further education: training, monitoring, assessment, accreditation and evaluation. *Mentoring and Tutoring*, **2** (3), 25–31.

UEL (1995 a) *Quality Manual*.

UEL (1995 b) *Quality Digest* Issue 3, July.

UEL (1995 c) *Student Guide*.

Warnock, M. (1978) *Special Educational Needs*. London: HMSO.

Wolfendale, S. (1992) *Institutional Support for Students' Learning. Towards a Cooperative Enterprise*. SCED Paper 70 (Standing Conference on Educational Development). Birmingham: SCED.

Wolfendale, S. (1994a) *Policy on Learning Support: Faculty of Science and Health: Booklet of Guidance for Faculty Staff*. London: UEL.

Wolfendale, S. (1994b) Participant learning in educational psychology training. *Educational and Child Psychology*, **11** (1), 75–84.

2

Learning development in HE: deficit or difference?

Robert Simpson

A number of significant factors are influencing the current and future nature of HE. A positive strategic response is required which recognizes the different levels of knowledge, skills and personal qualities that students, in ever increasing numbers, are now bringing to their HE learning experience. In this way, we can move away from the deficit view that sees the learning development needs of students as problems, synonymous with falling standards and requiring remedial provision, towards a more positive strategic response that aims to exploit the rich diversity of our students' experience, skills and knowledge. This chapter proposes a framework for learning support which embraces the widening range of different student experience and which can help to raise the quality of the student's total learning experience.

THE CHANGING UNIVERSITY

Those of us currently working in the HE sector are very much aware of the difficulties involved in ensuring a quality service for our students in the context of increasing numbers and decreasing resources. The changing nature of the student profile and the demands for greater accountability regarding the quality of the service HE provides are putting the current arrangements under strain. The higher education sector is committed to providing the highest possible quality of education while subjected to the close scrutiny of the Higher Education Funding Council for England (HEFCE) and the Higher Education Quality Committee (HEQC) through quality assurance monitoring mechanisms. Additional pressure to be more accountable comes from the Department for Education and Employment (DFEE), the National Union of Students (NUS) Charters and locally through individual university charters.

The irony of the present situation is not lost on those who have to deliver. At a time of significant reductions in full-time staffing levels, at the University of East London (UEL) from 1520 academic and support staff in 1970 to 1112 in 1995, the increase in student numbers has been dramatic, at UEL from 6726 full-time and part-time to 12,400 in 1995. Nationally, student numbers have risen to 1.3 million in the past ten years. In addition to this 'double whammy', the demand for greater accountability requires closer diagnosis of the nature of the student's total learning experience. It is a time of great change which calls for adjustment and new thinking. This rapidly evolving situation carries implications not only for the content of the curriculum but also for its delivery. Timetable space has to be created in the curriculum to acknowledge the learning development entitlement of students. This would involve a change of perspective on the part of the HE sector.

This chapter argues for a positive and strategic response which recognizes the different levels of knowledge, skills and personal qualities that the growing number of students are bringing to their HE learning experience. It recaps on some of those developments – now a feature of the HE sector – which are reinforcing the need for a shift in the way learning is acknowledged and it examines what this shift would involve with specific reference to the learning development needs of our students. It then details the essential features to be incorporated within an institutional learning development framework which would give greater priority to the learning development needs of its students and aim to improve participation and completion rates.

A number of factors can be seen as contributing to the present uncertainties; at the same time they highlight the need for a shift of perspective. First, there is the continuing debate about alleged falling standards, easier A-level exams and lax HE entry requirements. The case of the science don reflecting in the *Guardian Education Supplement* (12 September 1995) that his department 'was admitting considerable numbers of people who would not previously have entered or considered higher education', could be seen as reflecting the movement from an élite to a mass HE system. What is more pertinent to this discussion, is when he goes on to say that 'maybe sixty or seventy per cent of them, perhaps more, are really struggling'. Evidence supports the view that HE can no longer assume that all students bring the requisite skills to participate in and succeed at what is being asked. Whether this is due to the inadequacies of the students or the receiving institutions, HE is certainly having to rethink how it is supporting students. What are the implications of improving the overall quality of the learning environment to achieve higher participation and attainment levels? There is a danger that the debate surrounding standards will distract from the underlying issue of how the needs of present-day students are met within a mass system.

Second, there is the changing student profile. At UEL growing numbers of students are entering our institution with increasingly diverse backgrounds and expectations. Our mission states a commitment to encourage people from local communities to study at the university and to continue to widen access for mature students, those non-traditionally qualified and ethnic minority students. The statistics reflect the reality. Over sixty per cent of our students are mature, with forty-five per cent over the age of 25, and over fifty per cent are from ethnic communities. Forty per cent are recruited from local boroughs and seventy per cent from the Greater London area. In practical terms, the widening of access means that there is a growing number of students with increasingly diverse backgrounds and varied educational experience and expectations. A number of characteristics of such a profile can be identified:

- long absence from education
- mixed previous education experience
- a breadth of experience
- gaps in knowledge
- unpreparedness for HE
- lack of clarity about what is required
- early anxieties
- lack of confidence
- increasing outside commitments/pressure on time management
- linguistic diversity, and
- unfamiliarity with the UK system and academic conventions.

In addition, the domestic/financial situation of many students in the 1990s demands patterns/modes of study which do not allow, in their eyes, the luxury of a three-year total immersion. The design and delivery of the curriculum has to adjust to meet the needs of the different constituencies now entering universities. With such a profile of students, rich in characteristics that constitute potential fragmentation, the need to work, provide childcare and meet family responsibilities, etc., places a demand on the ability of older students to integrate their lives, inside and outside the institution, with formal education.

Changing modes of study are critically dependent on different modes of learning support. The situation is further complicated by the diversification of entry qualifications. It is an inescapable fact that HE is no longer dealing exclusively with students who have travelled the A-level entry route or arrive carrying a complete cocktail of learning. HE is no longer the preserve of a privileged minority. Diversification of the post-16 educational curriculum has resulted in a whole range of alternative access routes and qualifications. As Bimrose and Brown (1992, p.2) point out when discussing the criteria which should be used to determine entry into HE:

> Not only are there major changes in the policy context, but 'bottom up' curricular change also means that patterns of experience of applicants to higher education have become increasingly diverse. Additionally, there are also major differences in the context within which admissions tutors operate according to institution and subject area.

Given this profile, the need for a positive strategic response to meet learning development demands is increasingly being felt.

Third, the more recent developments in modularization have highlighted key issues of the quality of the students' total learning experience, in particular the key issue of how to maintain a sense of coherence. Courses and Programmes of Study (PoS) have to go beyond their own internal coherence. Students can no longer rely on coherence being provided by any one PoS, subject module or unit. Cognate disciplines do not function in isolation and coherence has to be evident at the programme and institutional levels. Modularization has raised to the surface issues of assessment, guidance and support and the coherence of the individual student's learning experience. The impact of this change has to be reflected within the curriculum (Symonds, 1995, p.14). 'What appeared to offer choice and flexibility began to seem like a recipe for less variety and a lot of fragmentation.'

This quote, from an article in which a second-year student at the University of Bradford reflects on the effects of modularization and semesterization at her own university, raises the question 'Do the changes in the organization of the curriculum brought about by modularization and semesterization challenge students to learn or do they merely encourage them to take bite sized chunks of learning?' The article illustrates how managers, in pursuit of certain institutional objectives, can impose the different demands of a unitized curriculum without questioning the implications for the methods of teaching, notions of coherence and quality. The range on offer has increased, from 80 to over 150 courses at UEL during the past twenty-five years, but is the offer significantly different or are we offering more of the same? The proliferation of courses does not automatically signify an improved product. You cannot have modularization and semesterization without clear strategies for curriculum design.

Given the changes in mass that have been taking place in HE over the past ten years, modularization and semesterization can be seen as having highlighted questions that required answers long ago. If one of the effects of their introduction is that we are asking ourselves afresh who students are and what it is that HE is offering, so much the better. This shift in perspective moves the discussion from the purely organizational frame back to the learning needs of the learner. It is not a bi-polar argument between coherence without choice, signified by the single honours degree, and choice without coherence, in some form of cafeteria style pick-'n'mix system. In categorizing the need for (pre-)entry, on-programme and exit guidance, the Robertson Report (1994) advocates the use of negotiated learning agreements and a PoS, 'finally negotiated with, and authenticated by, an appropriate academic authority' (p.276). What is being proposed within this discussion, is to broaden the discursive concepts of coherence and assessment so that they rest within a framework for educational guidance which in turn takes into consideration any specific institutional profile, Learning Development, and quality embedded within the 'total student experience' against which an institution like UEL measures itself in terms of audit.

Additionally, the growth in numbers and the decreasing unit of resource has meant that the personal tutor system – traditionally the vehicle for addressing individual learning needs – has come under stress to the point of collapse (Rivis, 1994, p.5). 'The personal tutor system was found to be under increasing strain in some universities because of the dramatic increases in the number of students.'

One demonstrable feature of the current 'strain' is that education guidance and support are varied and inequitable, further illustrating how the students' learning experience can become even more fragmented. However, it seems from this data (collated from 69 universities) that all has not been well with the personal tutoring system for some time. In this changing world, assessment is no longer a matter of the individual module/unit organizing its own internal arrangements; the standards demanded by any one module must refer to the wider context of the students' total learning experience. The ability of students to construct their own Programmes of Study and make them coherent can only be done with academic support and a systematic guidance structure. A framework of educational guidance is vital in making the overarching links. It is no accident that the effects of both modularity and mass expansion are being perceived as synonymous with the decline of the personal tutor system.

A DEVELOPMENTAL MODEL OF SUPPORT

Given the changed circumstances outlined above, how can HE resolve the present dilemmas and adopt a positive strategic response? A significant shift in perception is required to effect a solution. First of all, the characteristics of the present-day student profile means that individuals will have varying degrees of competence and performance required in the formal academic HE context. The difficulties students encounter are too often viewed from a deficit model position which proposes remedial provision to address perceived deficiencies in a student's previous education, ability or suitability for a programme. The durability of such views could owe their origins to the many versions of deprivation theory which have been offered to explain educational failure and which have persisted down the years. This has surfaced in the notions of cultural and verbal deprivation, vigorously attacked by Labov (1969) in the US in his article 'The logic of non-standard English'. Labov argued (p.179)

> There is no connection between non-standard English dialects and lack of ability in concept formation and that verbal deprivation theories can easily become self-fulfilling prophecies further hindering the scholastic achievement of ethnically different backgrounds.

Such notions have underpinned interventionist compensatory educational programmes across the world since the 1960s (Stubbs, 1980).

The second shift in perception needed is for staff to recognize that they have a responsibility for the development of students' overall development and not just the specificities of their own cognate discipline specialism. The Bullock Report, *A Language for Life* (1975), highlighted the importance of language across the curriculum and emphasized the need for all teachers to take a pro-active approach to developing the language ability of pupils in secondary schools. Over ten years later, an FEU occasional paper, *Language For All* (1986, p.3) stressed that 'All teachers are teachers of language whether or not they recognise the fact ... many see themselves as teachers of specialised academic and vocational subjects; improving students' language ability is often seen as someone else's responsibility.' This double shift in perception will go a long way towards HE institutions developing an ethos where the learning development needs of its students are seen as a vital element of the delivery of the learning entitlement of its students.

The Further Education Unit (FEU) in its 1993 document (p.11) *Supporting Learning – Promoting Equity and Participation* defines the notion of Learning Entitlement as 'All learners are entitled to a range learning opportunities which will enable them to fulfil their learning goals and ambitions and improve their life chances.' Within this context, an HE institution can analyse how this learning development component is delivered in practical terms. Learning development entitlement recognizes that students are entitled to develop their learning at any level in the mainstream curriculum. Hurley (1994, p. 13) explains what this means:

> It defines the student's learning needs from the situation of the student, the overall development of a student's learning skills, the demands of a learning programme, the levels of study, the demands of assessment and the teaching methods used. It is important to note that it is not only concerned with improving an individual's skills, but also with reviewing the demands imposed by the organisation of the curriculum and the methods of teaching.

Learning development systems encourage students to develop skills to participate and succeed. If we recognize that learning takes place everywhere, the trick is in the attempt to assess or measure the integrative process.

Essential to this more positive focus is the recognition that the responsibility to identify this entitlement does not rest solely with the student; the institution has a significant role to play in diagnosing and responding to the overall learning needs of its students. There are a number of documents that detail student entitlement such as the DFE HE Charter (Department for Education, 1993) which concentrates in large part on standards of service relating to student entitlement and the NUS Charter (1993) which covers much the same ground but also includes two papers dealing specifically with learning and teaching 'The Right to Good Teaching' and 'A Right to Learner Agreements'. Our own student charter at UEL is quite specific. The section '*We will offer you effective management of your learning*' states: 'We aim to provide structured opportunities for learning development for all our students, which recognise your prior learning and experience and which respect your language and culture' (1993, p.3). The institution has a role to play in the process: it must be explicit about the demands made by the organization of its curriculum and its methods of teaching and assessment. Effective diagnosis of an individual student's learning requirements is dependent on the assessment of the demands of the chosen PoS. In this process, staff teams would be expected to analyse the learning demands of their programmes.

More effective diagnosis of student needs – and the greater attention to the analysis of course demands – needs to be backed up by systematic support. Charters tend to focus on those aspects of a student's entitlement that relate to the rights of the student as customer. Other aspects of a student's life that clearly impinge on the effectiveness of their learning – such as finances, childcare and domestic responsibilities and arrangements and problems of a personal nature – are catered for within the broader learner support context and there will be services with clear roles within the institution. However, it is important to establish a clear institutional response – one that distinguishes between learner and learning support and the resources needed at course, programme and institutional levels – to ensure that learning development is delivered at the course and programme levels including mechanisms for providing the additional support some students will need.

Table 2.1 is adapted from the 'Taxonomy of College Services' in the FEU document *Learner Support Services in Further Education* (1993a). It illustrates the delivery of learning development located within an institutional learner support framework and clarifies the important distinction between the learner and learning. Such a model locates the delivery of aspects of learning development entitlement within a learner support framework. In this way, the personal tutor system – traditionally the vehicle for addressing individual learning needs and which has come under stress to the point of collapse – can be given a clearer role and fresh purpose. The first column identifies the learner *services*, the third column identifies the *resources* required to support learning and the central column identifies the *delivery* of learning development. The different elements listed in the central column receive priority during each of the four stages of a student's academic life: pre-entry, entry, on-programme and at exit.

Table 2.1 illustrates how learning development occupies a central space in an institution's learner support framework and is pivotal to delivering a high-quality learning experience. All students will have varying degrees of learning development needs which should be met as part of an institution's mainstream provision and responsibilities. The FEU document (1993b, p. 11) *Supporting Learning: Promoting Equity and Participation* introduces the notion of additional support which targets 'at risk' students. 'Some

Table 2.1: *Learner support framework*

Learner Services	Learning Development	Learning Resources
	ENTRY	
	Records of Achievement	
	(ROAs)	
	Guided admissions	
	APEL/assessment &	
	accreditation	
	Induction	
	Initial assessment	
	Skills audit	
	ON-PROGRAMME	
Student services	Tutorial support	Library services
Counselling	Personal/professional	Learning centres
Health/welfare	development	Open Learning facilities
Catering	Profiling	Study centres
Childcare	Recording achievement/	Resource based
Accommodation	progress reviews	learning
Overseas student care	Action planning	Computer networks
Financial services	Concurrent experiential	IT facilities
Access funds	learning	Multi-media technology
Recreation	Careers Education Unit	Learning packages
Registry	Key skills	Audio-visual aids
Careers	Transferable skills	
Student Union	Additional support	
	Subject-specific	
	curriculum workshops	
	EXIT	
	Exit guidance	
	Progression counselling	
	Transfer documentation/	
	transcripts	
	ROAs	

learners will require specific, *additional support* in order to help them meet these goals and to allow them to participate and achieve fully' [my emphasis]. Just as with learning development, its aim is to help students to progress towards and achieve their learning goals but the need for additional support may arise from a learning difficulty, a disability or a literacy, numeracy or language support requirement. Such a model has advantages not only for the student but also the institution, for it can help to achieve a higher quality of a student's total experience. It demonstrates the way in which Learner Support can be organized within an institution and locates roles and tasks for the effective delivery of academic guidance and support. The importance of recognizing and meeting the varying learning development needs of all students at all stages of their HE experience is recognized by such key aspects as diagnosis, action planning, the recording of progress and tracking of students.

This model would put into effect an institutional Learning Development framework and would achieve one of the chief recommendations of the Robertson Report (1994): redeployment of resources to ensure better quality educational guidance. It would assist academic performance in establishing a method of guidance – which would incorporate a wider role for assessment – and help to establish coherence. The wider context of assessment as a learning mechanism in itself, as well as its relationship to the cognate subject discipline, is vital in any institution which aims to provide lifetime learning, learning entitlement and learner enablement. This wider interpretation of assessment includes, but goes beyond, the often instrumental volume of summative end-of-module assessment and forms part of a more integrative programme. This details a student's total experience in relation to the institution and their academic studies and is performed iteratively throughout their progress until the final award. Assessment as a learning mechanism takes the form of needs analysis, action planning, profiling records, reflective diaries and summaries, together with a range of documentation appropriate to the different activities and phases of a student's HE experience. Such an approach answers many of the current questions being raised by HEFCE and HEQC – by which institutions are assessed and audited for purposes of quality control – but space within the curriculum is needed to encourage such developments.

In the same way as academics should keep hold of what they rightly see as key pointers in the maintenance of coherence within a subject area and cognate subject discipline, space must also be provided for students to understand the processes they have undergone within and beyond the institution, in relation to past lives, present disciplines and future objectives. The support function is to weld these processes together, academic assessment and self-assessment for learning development and lifelong learning. Tony Wailey (in Chapter 3) outlines how a wider interpretation of the function of AP(E)L can be used to integrate guidance and learning development in the academic context. He illustrates how the assessment focus of experiential learning is linked to learning development by making a case for the broader interpretation of educational guidance; one that accommodates wider notions of academic coherence and assessment and that not only fits within a modular system but also articulates wider personal and academic objectives. To be successful within this process there needs to be an iterative model of guidance at all levels within the university programme; then students and academics can address not only the coherence of specific modules but the overall programme coherence within a university's offer. This coherence is related not only to the learning that the student brings to the programme but the assessment of the totality of his or her learning in relation to the institution. 'Universities should not be supermarkets. Students are unlikely to be the best judges of standards and coherence. The ability to make such judgements is precisely what they have come to university to acquire' (NUS, 1993, p.2). Clearly, the responsibility does not rest solely with the student; the institution has a key role to play.

IMPLEMENTATION

All of the discussion so far, points to the need to implement systems which can encourage the effective delivery of learning development within an institution. The rest of this chapter outlines some of the essential features of any developments that constitute a positive strategic response to improve the overall quality of the learning environment to achieve higher participation and attainment levels. These features would include:

- Acceptance of the principle that *all* students can expect their learning needs to be met and that any one institution has an obligation to meet those expectations.

  Clear policy statements are required that commit the institution to providing for the learning development entitlement of its students and the additional support that some require.
- The delivery of the learning development needs of our students placed firmly within an *entitlement* model which defines the student's development needs from the situation of the student.

  It is not only concerned, with improving students' skills, but also with reviewing the demands imposed by the organization of the curriculum and the methods of teaching.
- All staff have a responsibility to develop and support students' learning within a positive learning environment.

  At the same time, the delivery of learning development, in particular that of additional support, requires trained staff.
- HE recognizes that learning development is not a peripheral

concern but core provision and that policies and practice place the student at the heart of the provision.

This has the advantage of meeting the demands of government charters and quality assessments which are placing greater priority on learning development issues.

- Courses, programmes and institutions have to ask how they are meeting the learning development entitlement of their students at four key points of the student experience:
  1. pre-entry (application/interview/advice)
  2. entry (admission/induction)
  3. on-programme (key and transferable skills)
  4. exit (employment).
- A model adapted and developed to deliver learning development entitlement within a framework of learner support, i.e. a mechanism for the effective delivery of a student's learning development entitlement through the integration of academic guidance and learning development support.

  The aim has to be to ensure that students are recruited for the appropriate programmes, that they are assessed and inducted, and that they stay and succeed.
- Assessment can no longer confine to the narrow role of assessing only subject discipline knowledge but takes on a wider role, particularly in the diagnosis and assessment of students' learning development entitlement.
- Assessment of the learning development needs of our students involve a structured assessment and recognition of prior learning and the drawing up of action plans.
- The function of learning development assessment is not simply to credit learning but also to diagnose needs.

  The diagnostic assessment of applicants establishes individual learning requirements but, equally important, it assesses the demands of the PoS applied for. The purpose of any assessment of threshold levels should be developmental and not discriminatory, i.e. not for the purpose of exclusion.
- Subject area teams analyse their programmes in terms of the learning demands to participate in and successfully complete them.

A commitment to these principles would mean a university providing a learning development framework covering literacy, numeracy, information technology, key learning skills and transferable skills appropriate to the level of learning. A coherent and positive strategy is one that aims to meet the learning development needs of students through the various stages of their HE lives. Clear policy statements are required that commit institutions to provide for the learning development entitlement of its students and the additional support that some require. To repeat: the aim is to ensure that students are recruited for the appropriate programmes, that they are assessed and inducted, and that they stay and succeed. The wider forms of assessment that this requires presuppose wider forms of support and explicit strategies for providing learning development at the course, programme and institution level. Such a model also demands effective tracking mechanisms to monitor and measure a student's progress. Implementation is dependent on supportive senior management within the institution and changes in prioritizing existing allocations from the external funding body.

CONCLUSION

To create the curriculum space needed, there would need to be a deliberate shift in the way that learning is acknowledged plus a fresh consensus as to what HE is offering its students. This is inextricably linked to finance. The NUS Charter (1993) highlights funding as a key issue:

> ... One of the main problems in higher education at present is underfunding ... one area where underfunding is increasingly becoming a problem is student support services. In many, though not all, institutions funding for student services has failed to keep pace with the increasing numbers of students. Further, many of the non-traditonal students entering higher education are likely to use such support services more intensely. Adequately funded support services are integral to the quality of education.

To implement the model proposed in this article is a pointless exercise, unless backed up by base-line funding. The traditional approach based on enrolment, 'bums on seats', has in the past encouraged the formulation of strategic and operational plans centred around the subject curriculum. However, changes in funding methodology towards a target-led enrolment base balanced by the key factors of retention, completion and achievement funding, would create a possible space within this hegemony for learning development entitlement. Educationalists need to use this space – this opportunity – to encourage and rationalize the shift by putting forward resource arguments. Exploiting this space makes financial sense because it protects the investments of the resource managers: the students. The changes in the FEFC methods of funding in recent years have certainly helped to shift the dominance of the knowledge-led curriculum and created the space for more attention to the processes involved in acquiring and using knowledge.

Crucially, it makes sound economic sense. To ignore these issues is short-sighted; institutions rely on high retention rates and high degrees of success in order to reach expected target funding. This model can go a long way to ensure that students are recruited on the appropriate programmes, that they are assessed and inducted, that they stay and succeed. Students stand to benefit and we, as educationalists, can feel confident that we are involved in higher quality provision which meets the wider range of students who are now gaining access to our institutions.

REFERENCES

Alderman, G. (1993) Boarding the space module, *Guardian*, 10 November, pp. 2–3.

Bimrose, J. and Brown, A. (1995) Skills and qualities required for entry into Higher Education in England: current practice and future policy. Paper presented at the 18th International Conference of the International Association for Educational Assessment, Dublin, September.

Bullock, A. (1975) *A Language for Life*. Report of the Committee of Inquiry appointed by the Secretary of State for Education and Science. London: HMSO.

Department for Education (1993) *The Charter for Higher Education*. London: DFE.

Education Guardian (1995) One academic is certain that expansion has led to falling standards. 12 September, 2–3.

FEU (1986) *Language for All*. London: FEU.

FEU (1993a) *Learner Support Services in Further Education*. Kettering: Staples Printers.

FEU (1993b) *Supporting Learning: Promoting Equity and Participation*. Dorset: Blackmore Press.

HEQC, (1995) *Guidelines for Guidance and Learner Support*. London: HEQC.

Hurley, J. (1994) *Supporting Learning*. London: Publications Department, The Staff College and Learning Partners.

Labov, W. (1969) The logic of non-standard English. In P.P. Giglioli (ed.) *Language and Social Context*. Harmondsworth: Penguin Education.

NUS (1993) *NUS Student Charter*. London: NUS.

Rivis, V. (1994) *Learning from Audit*. London: HEQC.

Robertson, D. (1994) *Choosing to Change*. London: HEQC.

Stubbs, M. (1980) *Language and Literacy: The Sociolinguistics of Reading and Writing*. London: Routledge.

Symonds, K. (1995) Personal view. *TES*, 21 April, p.14.

UEL (1994) *Student Charter*. London: Communications and Publicity Office.

3

Developing the reflective learner: Learning development entitlement and AP(E)L

Tony Wailey

Current AP(E)L practice is used principally to credit learning but, in the current context of learning support in HE, it will be used to play a more significant role in the diagnosis of the nature of the student's 'total learning experience'. To achieve this, this chapter suggests a wider interpretation of the function of AP(E)L, with greater emphasis on assessment and less on accreditation. In this way, it becomes a mechanism for the effective delivery of a student's entitlement through the integration of guidance and learning development support.

SETTING THE SCENE

The current debates – about power, the role of knowledge and critical theory within models of reflective learning which lie at the heart of the assessment of prior experiential and certificated learning, and AP(E)L – in turn illustrate what was intended to be a large learner-centred activity. This, derived from American community experience and European critical thought in terms of legitimacy and personal interests (Habermas, 1974), showed the capability of adult learning in all forms of education.

Since the advent of the National Council for Vocational Qualifications (NCVQ) in 1986, and notwithstanding such progressive terminology as 'empowerment' and learner 'autonomy' the term APL has become synonymous with accreditation. Its code has become one of accreditation. The outcome-driven mechanism of the NCVQ procedures have had a notable effect upon higher education, notably within the new universities. On many vocational-based programmes, behavioural objectives have become entwined with liberal pedagogic thought which has often resulted in the power of competence to discipline its own subject within their own area (Edwards and Usher, 1994).

Commentators point to a 'cult of credentialism' (Blackman and Storan, 1991) that often becomes enmeshed with new developments relating to modularization. AP(E)L as a set of measurable outcomes, or within a particular cognate discipline, has become synonymous with a particular module or clusters of modules; it then becomes merely a ticking off or mapping exercise. This, in practice, has led to AP(E)L being seen simply as a fast track route for professionals which, in a market environment, has often promoted systems inimical to the original conceptions of learner-centred activity.

Even the Council for National Academic Awards (CNAA), in establishing such initiatives as Credit Accumulation and Transfer Scheme in 1986, had reservations about sudden expansionism via this route and sought reassurance in pilot studies of AP(E)L in higher education (Storan, 1987; Evans, 1988; Robertson, 1994) which it realized would give institutional legitimacy to what had previously been peripheral or access type activity. Therefore, in seeking to identify areas of significant learning experienced by mature students, it is important to recognize that AP(E)L is not just about delivery to, or implementation of, competence-based systems; nor is it harnessing adult learning to a particular template of university modular delivery.

What is conceivable is that learners have learned a great deal but are unable to formulate this learning into university requirements. AP(E)L, in a learner support context, is only about recognizing the different arenas of that learning; it also becomes a powerful tool as a learning dynamic in itself, in order to best assist students with a particular Programme of Study (PoS). This works best within a group context and is very different from the context of AP(E)L schooling potential students into a dominant paradigm which 'regulates and farms adults through a process of self regulation' (Edwards and Usher, 1994, p.12). Neither does it fall into the morass of learner autonomy or empowerment, which can often be *non sequiteurs* for 'sink or swim' expansionism. At the heart of the matter is the purpose of assessment itself. AP(E)L within the context of learner support serves as a vehicle for demonstrating the coherence of each students' PoS, by support of a three-fold model of assessment: a diagnosis of the student's learning needs and achievements, a measure of the demands of the academic disciplines they are to study, and recognition of the inter-relationship of student-determined outcomes of learning and the outcomes of the academic programme. Within this context, AP(E)L is not just a systems-driven mechanism for credit; it is an essential ingredient to learner support, focusing as it does on learner-centred activities. These are integral to learning development entitlement within an increasingly fragmented curriculum. This concern with coherence has already been alluded to by Robert Simpson in Chapter 2.

This chapter seeks to reclaim the role of assessment within prior learning and to locate it firmly within a paradigm of learning support and diagnosis so that students may acquaint themselves better with the demands they face when confronted by HE at whatever point and by whatever mode they enter. This embraces not only local mission statements and strategic planning objectives (which embrace ideals of opening the doors of HE to those traditionally excluded) but the central tenet of AP(E)L policy at the University of East London (UEL) which follows the CNAA's orginal initiative 'to recognize learning from whatever its source' without predicating the outcome. This celebrates the greater diversity of qualifications and experiences which increased numbers of 'non-traditional' students' bring without relegating those experiences to 'deficit' models of learning. This is the effective assessment capacity of AP(E)L (the broader assessment capacity) that returns it to a learner-centred system; as such AP(E)L then becomes a diagnostic tool for learner support and development, to reconfigure assessment and locate it within the field of learner support, which in turn assists learner development.

ASSESSMENT OF PRIOR EXPERIENTIAL LEARNING (AP(E)L): DEFINITIONS

It is worthwhile at this point to revisit some of the definitions of AP(E)L captured by some of the pioneering work of the Learning from Experience Trust (Deardon, 1993). To paraphrase:

> APL is not the same as AP(E)L: APL is 'certificated' learning, implying a qualification usually obtained at the end of formal study; AP(E)L is 'uncertificated' learning, implying the absence of a qualification. APL is the assessment of prior learning and can be defined as the accreditation of previously acquired certificated learning. The term APL is also used as a generic acronym to cover both certificated and uncertificated learning. AP(E)L is the assessment of prior experiential learning which can be defined as the process by which appropriate uncertificated learning is recognized and given academic value. Experiential learning can be described as the knowledge,

skills and personal qualities acquired through life, work experience and study which are not formally attested.

The reality of AP(E)L is that many candidates – for assessment of academic credit towards a qualification – claim learning of both types and, for them, the process begins with the academic evaluation of their certificated learning and moves on to the assessment of their uncertificated or experiential learning.

General credit may be awarded to a student for activities which are recognized as being of academic value at the appropriate level. The credit recognized does not relate to any course on which the student is registered but is an academic judgement expressed in credits on the achievement of prior learning.

Specific credit may be awarded towards the attainment of a specific PoS. This is any type of general credit which is seen as being sufficiently relevant to count towards the award for which the student is registered.

In practice, because of quality judgements, there is considerable debate between the apportioning of general credit to specific credit. This raises the issue of portability of credit between institutions and the 'culture' of specific programmes. More importantly, as Boud *et al.* (1993, p. 83) point out, this raises another question about the relationship between assessment and accreditation: (Boud, Cohen and Walker, 1993, p.83) 'We cannot tell in advance what knowledge we will make our own … learning from experience is often far more indirect than we pretend it to be. It is not a simple, rational process.'

Many definitions of AP(E)L concern themselves principally with accreditation without noting that these are assessment processes in the first instance. If we look at the purpose of assessment in learning development, we find that the diagnosis of need is primary and linked to the assessment demands of a particular PoS. AP(E)L and learning development meet at the primary focus of assessment as seen in the development of a student's learning skills in relation to the demands of a learning programme and the integration of this process into particular levels of study. Within a learning development framework, AP(E)L raises the question of where exactly assessment/diagnosis of need begins, continues and ends as seen from different perspectives of an individual's learning curve.

Viewed in this manner, AP(E)L and learning development share similar purposes in assessment and are not exclusively concerned with accreditation. In many instances, notably the extremely successful UEL–Ford Motor Company engineering programme, AP(E)L is only brought into operation as an extension of an admissions procedure. As in the case of learning development it should also have a preparatory, monitoring, supportive and evaluative function throughout a student's time within HE. This aligns AP(E)L much closer to the guidance, mentoring and monitoring roles as outlined in the Robertson Report (1994) and SEEC (1994–1996) projects in the establishment of credit frameworks.

AP(E)L should not only be carried over into the curriculum; it should be concerned with how personal constructs of experience and learning can be credited mid-way through a PoS, e.g. how concurrent experiential learning is to be supported. This, in itself, would illustrate the number of ways in which learning and epistemological issues could be articulated, besides assisting students to note their own learning processes as well as the multi-interpretative paradigms which characterize learning in HE. AP(E)L is central to this process and so sits comfortably within the delivery of learning development.

LOCAL AND NATIONAL DEVELOPMENTS

Background

All those involved in the HE sector are aware that this is a period of significant change. Growing numbers of students are entering HE institutions with increasingly diverse backgrounds and expectations. At UEL our statistics support such observations: over 60 per cent are mature students, over 45 per cent are over 25 and more than 50 per cent come from ethnic communities. Coupled with this growth is the decreasing unit of resource. The HE world has changed and is continuing to change. HE has to recognize this different landscape without falling into the moral panic induced by sections of the 'quality' conservative press. This requires perspective transformations on the part of the university, i.e. it calls for a paradigm shift in the way that learning is acknowledged.

The long history of independent study at UEL pre-figured some of those moral panics and talk of deviancy from some specific norm; yet some of its most central concerns seem to be re-emerging within a new modularized system, that is in many ways the unreconstructed concern with 'holism' promoted within the school which sought to promote the coherence of subject, learning process and student as the central project. To recognize learning without particularly seeking to credit it, but rather to strengthen person-centred curriculum development via integration, balance, coherence and progression – these were the preoccupations of independent study.

In similar vein, admissions tutors were adept as assessing non-traditional students for possible entry and credit transfer (advanced standing). What was lacking was any diagnosis of student needs which often accompanied their non-formal learning. The dynamics of self diagnosis and assessment extend to those with formal qualifications as it lends the dynamics of learning support and reformulation to what were previously 'certificated' experiences. It caters for the difference implicit in such arrangements between different levels of experience. This was endorsed by our experiences with three very different cohorts of participants on three specific programmes.

One of those projects was a European Social Fund programme, 'APL for refugees'. Although this was a short intensive programme principally aimed at accrediting the prior experience and qualifications of mature students gained outside the British education system, it was immediately clear that the curriculum had to address both learning development and language development issues, before any articulation could be made in using credit systems.

At another level we were developing a model for personal and professional development (PPD) within a 'Certificate in teaching and learning in HE' (recently validated by the Staff and Educational Development Association) in which it had been found that AP(E)L was not particularly applicable unless attributed to the core modules of the programme. The PPD unit acts as the spine to the programme. It asks new lecturers to identify what they know already and to carry out a needs analysis while also taking 'snapshots' of their development and concluding with a reflective exercise in which they wrap up their experiences of the programme, but not their personal and professional development. The programme ends but their professional profile is ongoing throughout their professional lives.

A third project further endorsed these findings. A pilot project was undertaken to evaluate the HEQC guidelines, *Guidance and Learner Support for Quality Assurance*. A specific case study highlighted all the problems which characterize many vocational programmes when APL is purely the code for accreditation. The delivery of the AP(E)L Professional Studies in Nursing (PSN) 251 module in 1995, to two cohorts of post-RGN nurses applying to join the BSc Nursing Degree (formerly a Diploma programme) was a case in point. The students had to produce a personal profile/portfolio containing evidence of prior experiential and certificated learning as evidence to claim the 120 credits at Level 2 and thus to enable them to progress on to Level 3 of the degree, they also had to defend this portfolio with a separate 40-minute *viva voce* examination.

All three examples illustrate that there is no clear division between when assessment ends and when accreditation takes place. In one instance, we were dealing at Level O (pre-entry level) and in another at Level M (post-graduate) with the PSN 251 in the middle. More importantly, we were using the same methodology. The difference was the level of learning outcomes expected from the respective cohorts of participants. The question was how to integrate the methodology used in these three projects and how it could be applied at Levels 1, 2 and 3 within the undergraduate degree scheme (UDS). In short, where would this methodology interact with 'the totality of the student's learning experience' and importantly, how would it demonstrate the way in which guidance and learning development is managed within the whole institution? This is pertinent when considering the impact of modularization and the growing recognition that PoS have to go beyond the internal coherence of each subject module or unit. What became increasingly clear through working with these cohorts at such opposing levels was that AP(E)L and learning development models could usefully serve each other's different but mutual ends to implement such key aspects as diagnosis, action planning, the recording of progress and tracking of students – as well as the more formal accreditation.

The 'cult of credentionalism' has its own driving force and any new university would ignore it at its peril; yet, it is only the application of a wider assessment model that can address the diversity of students and develop their different experience. 'The quality of the total student experience is the benchmark by which we measure our performance in meeting your *legitimate* needs' [my emphasis] says UEL's student charter. What critical theorists associated with the Frankfurt School would have made of this statement is anyone's guess (Held, 1980). What is incontrovertible is that it is only within the context of curriculum change that the model below can facilitate all levels of advice and guidance within a framework of learning development. AP(E)L becomes central to this process.

THE AP(E)L MODEL IN PRACTICE: PROCESS AND OUTCOMES

The AP(E)L process within this context of pre-entry, on-programme and exit assessment involves four exercises and can operate at any level. The exercises are:

1. *position paper* – personal profile with needs analysis
2. *extended CV* based upon a specific taxonomy of learning achievement
3. *learning outcomes* – documented past and present academic achievements
4. *critical review* – a reflective learning exercise.

This process ends with a planning/exit exercise, an opportunity to analyse and reflect upon performance. Students, irrespective of the time spent on such an exercise, provide a completed portfolio which includes all four exercises detailed above. The portfolio provides a crucial point of reference for the monitoring of an individual's learning development, for establishing learning goals and strategies for their realization as well as for articulating the processes of critical reflection, credit and assessment that accords with a structured self-development programme at any level. The exercises are illustrated in more detail below.

Position paper

The self is central to the learning process. A position paper is based upon where the participants are coming from, where they are at present, where they hope to arrive and how they are going to achieve this. In many ways, this is an abbreviated version of a learning contract associated with the humanist cognitive perspective (Rogers, 1983; O'Reilly, 1993).

Example of a Personal Profile and Position Statement

I was born in Britain. I received the basic five-year primary and seven-year secondary schooling. While at school I had a weekend and holiday job as a domestic assistant in a psychiatric hospital (Runwell Hospital). As well as my domestic duties I used to help the nurses by feeding patients and helping them with general nursing care when they were short staffed. It was while I was working at the hospital I decided to be a nurse. I went straight from school to commence Nurse Training. I trained for three years at Southend General Hospital, receiving a very thorough training which prepared me well for my future career in nursing.

I worked as a Staff Nurse when I qualified in a busy Surgical Ward. I was responsible for twelve patients for their pre- and post-operative care. I left to have the first of my three sons. Following his birth, I worked as a Staff Nurse on an Ophthalmic Ward part-time from June 1975 to September 1976.

In September 1976, I was successful in obtaining a post as a School Nurse in a village. I had responsibility for a senior school, junior school and infant school. I started 'healthy living' talks to the children, educating them about healthy eating, hygiene and elementary sex education. I also had a caseload of elderly clients who I would visit for regular health checks. This was the beginning of my interest in care of the elderly.

In 1989, I commenced my present job as a Liaison Sister for Care of the Elderly. I liaise between the Hospital and Community Staff to ensure that the patients have a safe discharge home. A week following discharge, I visit them to ascertain whether they are maintaining the same level of independence as they had in hospital. I use my skills and knowledge to contact the appropriate services if the client is having problems. To assist in my work, I successfully completed the ENB 941 Nursing Elderly people in 1994.

At present, I am working as a Continence Adviser to Residential Homes, as well as my job as a Liaison Sister. My interest in continence started when I completed the ENB 978 Promotion of Continence and Management of Incontinence. I talk to the carers in the homes, advising them, encouraging the carers to do toileting programmes, and with the co-operation of the carers and the resident, we are successful in getting a resident with incontinence, continent. This is very rewarding to both the client and the carers. It is essential to encourage the carers, to get them interested and to talk to them about taking NVQ qualifications.

I am very interested in the NVQ. I believe it will become as important as traditional examinations. NVQ is theory and practice based. I am an Assessor for the NVQ Level II direct care award. I go into Residential Homes assessing YTS students on their practice. For this, I home into their personal skills to relate to young people. Another area I use my interpersonal skills is when I do bereavement visits to the elderly, which involves the skill of listening.

With my insight towards the needs of patients and families I know the knowledge I have relating to the Community would be an asset to the Health Visiting Team. I want to go forward and do my Health Visiting training. I have been successful in the face of many candidates of obtaining sponsorship. I hope to commence my BSc Honours Degree in Health Visiting at the University of East London.

To help me achieve this goal I will use my knowledge and

> skills I have gained from twenty-five years as a Nurse. It is
> with the completion of my portfolio that I hope to claim 120
> credits at Level II so I may commence the Level III study
> programme.

Such an exercise encourages students to begin the process of contextualizing their own learning experiences, and specifically, within the academic environment. This position paper model can be extended to allow students to make a claim for credit and more importantly to outline and assess what their past learning involved. It is in this context that the self is central to the learning process.

Extended CV

In the second exercise students analyse, by means of **an extended curriculum vitae**, what **skills, knowledge and personal qualities** they possess in relation to their work experience. This is based on taxonomies of skills and knowledge and focuses very much on the behaviourist philosophy of trying to identify systematic educational objectives which include affective learning (Carter 1985).

Example of an extended curriculum vitae

EMPLOYMENT
1980–1985 Private Music Teacher/Recorder Player
Job Description As a private teacher I offered lessons in recorder playing to children of all ages and adults. This involved preparing pupils for exams, competitions and performances. As well as individual lessons I also encouraged pupils to play and perform together and, to this end, organized ensembles and concerts. Also at this time I was able to do some performance work mostly in the field of early music and historical performances. Working with a group performing 14th- to 17th-century music on copies of original instruments.
Personal Qualities The ability to interact with a varied client base (from four-year-old prodigy to middle-aged executive looking for a new hobby). Personal motivation to work without college support. 'Salesmanship' to attract students and performance jobs.
Skills Organization of time, personal curriculums, concerts and festivals. Co-operation with parents. Evaluating an indi-

vidual's needs and negotiating with them a set of targets. Personal musical skills of performance.
Knowledge Technical knowledge of the instrument and playing techniques. Knowledge of both teaching and performance repertoire. Knowledge of requirements of exams.

This exercise indicates a progression from the personal profile to a more analytical framework with which students can demonstrate different forms of their learning. It is this sequencing of learning that benefits students approaching the rigour demanded by peer assessment, seminar papers, written assignments and those learning skills that HE demands of its students, regardless of level.

Learning outcomes

A switch in focus takes students to a third assignment which is based on a social constructivist approach to learning and describes the outcomes of specific work situations (Kolb 1984). It documents past and present learning outcomes. This model needs to be more prescriptive before the participants start to use assessment to determine their own learning situations.

Instructions: Study/Work-Based Learning Outcomes

Refer to David Kolb's *Learning Cycle*. You could also use this framework if you wished to incorporate any short courses you have undertaken and want to include within your portfolio:

Experience	Job which requires something of you.
Reflection	The special situation you find yourself in.
	The context which relates to the problem you encountered within your experience above.
Conceptualization	Problems encountered (list them from above) and can the student identify these problems in a different way?
Evaluation	What learning has come from this cycle?
	We would demonstrate this as learning outcomes.

You could then structure your study/work-based learning into:

(a)   a description of the job/programme
(b)   the specific situation of yourself to the job/learning programme
(c)   the problems you encountered and attempt to structure and re-structure
(d)   the learning outcomes that arise from 'evaluating' all of the above links in the cycle.

This outline will be helpful for anyone engaged in the assessment of prior learning, with its accompanying difficulties of identifying learning outcomes with the learner categorizing knowledge, skills and personal qualities, and extracting learning from experience in precise statements.

Critical review

By the end of the AP(E)L process, the student will have engaged with relevant prior learning, assessment and needs analysis of knowledge, skills and personal qualities, the integration of the learning outcomes from past and present experiences of study and work and the whole process of assessment issues concerning personal development. The overall analysis of this process will be finalized in the form of a 1500-word narrative, the reflective learning essay. The critical review requires students to reflect on and assess the process of the component parts of their PoS. It characterizes the different attributes of the programme and how the student has engaged with them to produce a final, summative evaluation. Such an evaluation can also serve as a synoptic planner for further development.

This personal learning report draws the different strands together. These exercises show the efficacy of an AP(E)L central strand to learner support in higher education. The position paper and the extended CV draw upon and value previous experience; they can identify weaknesses as well as strengths but more importantly they situate and contextualize experiences to and identify different areas of learning as witnessed in the critical review. This is not always evidenced in paper qualifications. It highlights the multi-interpretative paradigm that characterizes higher education.

IMPLEMENTATION OF THE MODEL

Table 3.1 sets out the possible components of the delivery of learning development and the AP(E)L process. The AP(E)L column itemises the four documents which go towards a student's final portfolio as described above. They correspond with the three key phases of a student's HE career, pre-entry, on-programme and exit column. The first column refers to the different skills that receive priority during the three key phases. The threshold skills are those identified by the programme as the ones needed to gain entry to a programme of study. The core skills are those that a student will need to participate fully and which will be addressed principally in the first year. By the end of the programme, the student will have developed the set of transferable skills that are expected of a graduate. The second column indicates some of the practical ways in which the learning development needs of students can be realized. These are the various elements which, by switching towards an academic guidance focus with more clearly defined activities and end results, would help to give a renewed function to the current personal tutor system which is struggling to stay alive.

Such a model has advantages not only for the student but also for the institution; it can help to achieve a higher quality of a student's total experience.

Table 3.1 *HE Learning Development*

Skills	Realizations	AP(E)L Documents	Phase
THRESHOLD	Records of admission Skills audit/diagnosis Action planning Learning agreement	1. Position paper 2. Extended CV	Pre-entry
KEY	Profiling Learning outcomes Additional Support Careers/Education Unit Monitoring and Tracking	3. Work-based learning outcomes	On-programme
TRANSFERABLE	Records of Achievement Progression Counselling Transcripts	4. Critical review Reflective learning Essay Personal learning Report	On-programme
		Portfolio	Exit

This wider model of AP(E)L goes beyond pure accreditation and actually helps the student to make sense of the learning experience, which also helps progress participation in the cognate discipline area. This returns us to the role of learning development and the threefold role of assessment.

The benefits are in early diagnosis and frameworking which links with pre(entry) guidance and focuses on goals and strategies to be achieved, the measurement of progress and control which reflects changing priorities on the route through HE and the development of analytical skills which balance the learning experience with former and future lives. Assessment has still to be fully utilized within the context of life-long learning; it is this reason why AP(E)L is seen here in the context of learner support.

These are similar benefits for the institution; indeed the recognition of different modes of learning are central to its survival. For UEL, Gosling (1995, p. 7) suggests that,

> Universities cannot afford to allow increasing failure and re-sit rates which widened access may bring. If standards are to be maintained without wasting resources, adequate academic guidance ceases to be an optional matter. Universities with more open policies cannot afford not to provide good learner support services. This issue is central to the achievement of cost effective, quality, higher education.

Within the context of AP(E)L linking with learning development in a wider framework of learner support, the benefits for the institution become easier to categorize. The guidance factor runs through a student's entire stay within HE; this reduces the dangers that fragmentation and different modes of study can bring. It also safeguards a standardized approach yet is adaptable to subject specific needs, with the guarantee of early assessment for individual student learning needs. It encourages course teams to analyse the learning development demands of their programmes and, at the same time, links services which support the learner from pre-entry to exit, guidance and afterwards into life-long learning. In short, it moves beyond a purely deficit model which focuses solely on retention and completion rates.

THE FUTURE

Features of the AP(E)L model to carry forward learning development within the learner support context include:

- role in admissions procedures
- identification of ongoing support
- shaping curriculum at all stages (pre-entry/on-programme/exit)

• coherence within module and semester systems
• redefinition of personal tutor role and academic guidance.

Assessment can no longer confine itself to its traditional role of assessing subject discipline knowledge; it must take on a wider role, particularly in the diagnosis and assessment of students' learning development entitlement. It is not just the students who are responsible for identifying this entitlement; the institution has a significant role to play in diagnosing and responding to the overall learning needs of its students. The success of a student's self-assessment depends on how explicit the institution is about the demands made by the curriculum and the methods of teaching and assessment.

This also returns us to the simple recognition that the system has to benefit individuals as well as vocational groups and academic institutions in terms of the primacy of learner support. The heartland of AP(E)L is the development of diagnosis and advice within the context of a learner-centred series of activities. This is based primarily on an audit of strengths and gaps in learning and the specific situations of students in relation to their learning. More importantly, it allows participants to construct bigger pictures where they themselves can assist in the production. Whoever writes the script is ultimately unimportant because, as we all know, that always changes along the way. The capacity to reflect, conceptualize and act is the key.

CONCLUSION

Local and national development

There is still much difference between the equitable and the economic within funding arrangements. However, the publication of National and Regional Guidelines on credit, guidance and learning support (Robertson, 1994; SEEC, 1995; Learning from Audit, 1994–96; HEQC, 1995) places a greater transparency on outlining the distinct needs of non-traditional students. Indeed the term itself is increasingly becoming redundant, as more and more diverse learning arrangements are presented for admission to the new universities.

UEL has played a role in piloting both local and national guidelines in the context of AP(E)L as learner support as well as an accreditation mechanism. The AP(E)L group of the SEEC Consortium has been meeting regularly since 1991 and has recently produced its own Code of Practice to reflect wider consideration of the issues in which UEL has fully participated. All of these developments serve to indicate the particularistic, local, regional and national concerns which impact upon mass HE and the increasingly central role of guidance and learner support within modularized systems of learning. HE is having to pay more attention to the learning development needs of students, but what are the implications for improving the overall quality of the learning environment to achieve higher participation and attainment levels? As one commentator suggested five years go (Mansfield, 1990), in relation to the cult of credentialism 'The whole system has to benefit individual as well as an "amorphous" nation and employers' organisations'.

An important part of the answer to this question rests with our ability to resolve the dilemma of meeting the learning needs of students within such a mass system by anticipating and predicting their portfolios of need and ensuring the development of their learning. If we recognize that learning takes place everywhere, the trick is in the attempt to measure and situate the integrative process through the reconfiguring of the modes of assessment within the academic timetable. AP(E)L as a process of learning development contributes to the students' total learning experience (within the curriculum) by providing the coherence of overarching links to each student's learning programme.

The strengths of the model are outlined above. To recapitulate, it has proved successful with many distinct vocational and educational groups, academic staff programmes and individual students within the university. As yet however, it has not been fully integrated within the totality of the undergraduate curriculum, nor in the management or assessment of curriculum space which it demands. In short, it does not fit except as servicing a series of discrete units within the modularized and semesterized timetable. The irony of this situation is precisely where the discussion was first joined in this chapter between viewing AP(E)L as merely a systems-driven accrediting system or, more profitably, locating it within a wider assessment nexus which attempts to support learning. Again the logical requirement is a reconfiguring of the assessment process to enable such a model to provide the overarching links to a student's learning at every level within and around the university.

It brings the current debates about power and knowledge and critical theory not only to students' self-assessment of their own learning but of that learning in its relationship to the multi-interpretative paradigms which characterize higher education. Institutions must decide what offer they must make in return when they have the capacity to reflect upon the relationship between knowledge and human activity. This leaves us with the larger vision to which AP(E)L has aspired in its support of all learning, rather than the methodological solipsism (Apel, 1972) which determines behaviour to objectify learner and cognate discipline. National, regional and local guidelines may make this task easier but it still remains for the local institution to determine its own offer. At UEL these questions are at least being asked.

REFERENCES

Apel, K.O. (1972) The priority of communication and foundation of the humanities. *Man of the World*, **5**, 10.

Atkins, M., Beattie, J. and Dockrell, W.B. (1993) *Assessment Issues in Higher Education*. Newcastle: Department of Education, University of Newcastle.

Assiter, A. and Fenwick, A. (1993) *Profiling in Higher Education*. London: Council for National Academic Awards.

Blackman, S. and Storan, J. (1991) *Experiential Learning*. Paper presented at the Second International Conference on Experiential Learning, Guildford, University of Surrey.

Boud, D., Cohen, R. and Walker, D. (1993) *Using Experience for Learning*. (Society for Research into Higher Education). Buckingham: Open University Press.

Carter, R. (1985) A taxonomy of objectives for professional education. *Studies in Higher Education*, **10** (2), 135–50.

Deardon, G. (1993) *The Potential of the Assessment of Experiential Learning*. London: HMSO.

Edwards, R. and Usher, R. (1994) Disciplining the subject: the power of competence. *Studies on the Education of Adults*, **26** (1), 12–13.

Evans, N. (1988) *Assessment of Prior Experiential Learning*. London: Council for National Academic Awards.

Gosling, D. (1995) *Academic Guidance and Learner Support*. Birmingham: Higher Education Quality Council.

Habermas, J. (1974) *Knowledge and Human Interest*. Oxford: Heinemann.

Held, D. (1980) *Critical Theory: Horkheimer to Habermas*. Stamford: University of California Press.

HEQC (1995) *Guidelines for Guidance and Learner Support*. London: HEQC.

Kemp, G. and McClelland, D. (1986) Executive competence: what characterises executive functioning among senior managers. In Steinburg, R. and Wagner, R. (eds) *Intelligence: Nature and Origins of Competence*. Cambridge: Cambridge University Press.

Kolb, D. (1984) *Experiential Learning*. Englewood Cliffs: Prentice-Hall.

Mansfield, R. (1990) *Values in Education and Training*. Rotherham: Business Development Partnerships.

Mezirow, J. and Associates (1990) *Fostering Critical Reflection in Adulthood*.

New York: Jossey-Bass.

O'Reilly, D. (1989) On being an educational fantasy engineer. In S. Weill and I. McGill (eds) *Making Sense of Experiential Learning* (Society for Research into Higher Education). Buckingham: Open University Press.

O'Reilly, D. (1993) Negotiating in an institutional context, In M. Laycock and J. Stephenson (eds), *Using Learning Contracts in Higher Education*. London: Kogan Page.

Robertson, D. (1994) *Choosing to Change*. London: Higher Education Quality Council.

Rogers, C. (1983) *Freedom to Learn*. Cleveland: Howell-Bell.

SEEC (South East England Consortium for Credit Transfer) (1995) *Towards a Regional Credit Framework*. Sheffield: Department of Employment.

Storan, J. (1987) *Making Experience Count*. London: Learning from Experience Trust.

Zuber-Skerritt, O. (1992) *Professional Development in Higher Education*. London: Kogan-Page.

4

Supporting students with specific learning difficulties (dyslexia)

Stella ni Ghallchoir Cottrell

INTRODUCTION

Support for dyslexic students is a recent phenomenon in the higher education sector, with a few outposts such as Bangor, South Lancashire and North London being among the first to offer support systems. Prior to the 1990s, most dyslexic university students either struggled through alone or dropped out, perhaps not knowing why they found certain aspects of study so difficult. Several developments this decade have radically altered the picture. More children whose difficulties have been recognized at school are applying to university, and expect some provision for their needs. There are more special needs tutors in FE trained (often in the south through the London Language and Literacy Unit) to recognize and support dyslexia. Universities taking a large proportion of students from FE, particularly from Access courses, have seen an increase in adults discovered to be dyslexic. Widening access policies in universities have probably also contributed to the increased numbers of dyslexic adults. Universities which advertise the benefits of revealing dyslexia, whether in terms of study support, disability allowances or alternative examination arrangements, have found students coming forward for help who were previously anxious to conceal their dyslexia. Two Higher Education Funding Council (HEFCE) projects on disability in HE (1993–95) have encouraged a blossoming of support for dyslexia within a number of universities (see also Cooper and Corlett, Chapter 10). In addition, a more widespread general awareness has led many people to come forward for assessment who previously had not considered that their difficulties might be attributable to dyslexia.

This chapter looks at the experiences of the University of East London (UEL) in trying to meet the needs of students with specific learning difficulties (dyslexia), and the effect of rising numbers on the services offered. The chapter covers everyday issues which may be encountered by any university aiming to establish support for dyslexic students: issues relating to definitions and 'labels', the kinds of difficulties students experience, referral procedures or how students access available assistance, principles informing the assessment of students, and the levels of support which have been possible. Four case studies will be presented to illustrate some of the variations in student experience and the kinds of support required in particular instances.

DEFINITIONS AND LABELS

Variety in the range, combination, degree, and intractability of difficulties from one person to another has meant that so far, there is no universal acceptance of any particular 'label' or definition or unitary explanation. Pumfrey and Reason (1991) give two pages of definitions. Dyslexia, literally, means 'difficulty with language'. However, it is clear that many 'dyslexic' people have additional difficulties which are not language related, and which may be more intractable than their language difficulties. It is also the case that reading difficulties in some people can be more obviously traced to visual difficulties such as unstable binocular control (Stein, 1994) or Meares-Irlen syndrome (Irlen, 1991), while, in others, auditory processing differences make phonetic tracking and decoding difficult (Miles and Miles, 1990). Some professionals, notably a number of educational psychologists, prefer the term 'specific learning difficulties' to encompass the range of difficulties displayed. Some practitioners eschew labels altogether and concentrate on the individual pattern of difficulties, strengths and needs.

At UEL, students express a preference for the term 'dyslexia'. 'Specific learning difficulties' is disliked on the grounds that it is a cumbersome phrase, hard to pronounce, and often confused with 'learning difficulties' in general. Some students argue that they do not have difficulties with learning; for them, it is their performance under time constraints that is at issue. Moreover, while students may emphasize their 'difficulties' in order to have their needs met, many feel that they have strengths which go unrecognized because of current modes of teaching and assessment. For example, dyslexic students often appear exceptional at rapid associations so that they can use small amounts of information to generate ideas or to arrive at a deep understanding of an issue.

They may excel at thinking visually, at creative writing, at design tasks, inventions, or converting information from 2–D to 3–D. The pattern of strengths identified fits well with research on dyslexic differences in brain organization, and the effects of that organizational difference on processing differently presented information for all sensory modalities (Stein, 1994).

Adults assessed as having specific learning difficulties (Dyslexia) typically describe a pattern of life difficulties. This usually includes difficulties with some or all aspects of written or spoken language, such as spelling, pronunciation, word retrieval, converting ideas into words, or keeping track of what is heard, said, read or written. Some students may have extreme difficulties decoding words as they read and make sense of passages by intelligent guess work from the look of a number of key words. Others may read quite fluently but find the effort of decoding detracts from their comprehension and memory of what they read. However, almost all of these students also indicate difficulties with their sense of time, certain aspects of memory, organizational skills, distinguishing between left and right, auditory or visual anomalies, and some kinds of physical co-ordination. They often describe themselves as clumsy. Some have had extreme reading difficulties in the past, but find organizational skills or physical co-ordination currently create life problems for them, some of which interfere with their studies. Ellis (1984) points out that action planning and speech are both associated with the left hemisphere, so it may be that difference or damage in that area of the brain underlies difficulties in language and organized action planning. Many dyslexics also appear to excel at skills which are associated with the right hemisphere, such as certain spatial skills. It may be the case that underlying differences in brain organization may help to account for the particular patterns of difficulties and strengths which dyslexics experience (Miles and Miles, 1990; Stein, 1994).

Newly diagnosed students are frequently shocked at how other people still react to the label 'dyslexia', assuming it means they cannot read at all, or see the world in reverse. Nonetheless, being diagnosed with a label can have very positive consequences. Many students say it has meant understanding themselves for the first time; it has led to at least some of their needs being met; it has enabled them to identify others and share experiences and strategies, and to form or identify organizations which can help.

THE EFFECTS OF NUMBERS

As there is no universally accepted definition of dyslexia or agreement about why it occurs, it is difficult to state the incidence of
dyslexia in the general population, but Thomson (1984, p.15) gives
a 'conservative estimate' of five per cent. Numbers of known and
assessed students at UEL, with a student body of 10,000, rose from
four new referrals in 1991 and 20 in 1992, to approximately 90 in
1994–95. It is expected that numbers are likely to stabilize at
approximately 300 overall, or three per cent of the student body.
Similar numbers are being reported from other universities which
advertise a dyslexia service.

The first dyslexic students who received support at UEL benefited from the small numbers then presenting themselves for help
– usually this was simply a request for study skills support. One
particular advantage of the small scale of operations was that the
student needed to liaise only with one member of staff for an
assessment of need, personal support with their studies, demonstrations of technology that could be of assistance, help with
applying for the Disabled Students Allowance (DSA), help with
learning to use technology, advice on how to access alternative
examination arrangements, and anything else which seemed to be
necessary. These services are still offered, but the student may now
need to see a different person for each service. However, because
dyslexia was a new HE phenomenon, many teaching staff did not
know how to respond and the experience for students was not
always very positive.

With an expectation of approximately three hundred dyslexic
students at the university at any one time, and without a commensurate rise of staff, very different support systems have had to
develop very quickly. This is, again, common to many universities
which have started a dyslexia service. At UEL, although the
service is co-ordinated from the Learning Development Unit,
many university staff and students are involved in aspects of
support work even if in very small ways, as is exemplified in the
case studies below. There is less bewilderment expressed now by
staff when students mention they are dyslexic. There is a wider
range of services and expertise available to students, financed
either by the university, the Higher Education Funding Council
(HEFCE) projects, or the DSA. However, from the students'
perspective, life as a dyslexic student is still a struggle; many
people misjudge them or can be rude or aggressive about dyslexia,
and the amount of support available can fall short of what is
needed.

IDENTIFICATION, DIAGNOSIS AND ASSESSMENT

In an ideal world, those who feel they experience study difficulties would be offered assistance irrespective of label or level of difficulty. Their progress would be monitored, the assistance altered to suit their needs or learning style and, if difficulties persisted, they might be referred on for more expert guidance, or formal assessment if necessary.

It is unlikely that many universities could finance such a model given present funding. Many find that their students' study needs outweigh available resources. Study skills workshops or drop-ins are often tokenistic, and do not address the shortfall in required study or language skills which is sometimes evident in the major part of the student body. Teaching staff and pastoral systems may be over-burdened. Tutors may have responsibility for many more students than previously, and sometimes contact is restricted to lecture halls with hundreds of students. The few pieces of written work marked before the onset of first semester exams are not, in general, sufficient to enable staff to identify patterns of difficulty or monitor progress.

Nonetheless, staff development, as well as the increased numbers of known dyslexic students, has raised awareness among teaching staff in some areas: approximately one third of dyslexia referrals are from course staff. Some students are encouraged by other dyslexic students to come for an assessment. Others come, initially, for study skills or support with academic English. Increasingly, students mention seeing publicity about dyslexia at UEL or hearing about it through radio or television. Students also ask for dyslexia assessments because they are struggling with their coursework or examinations: over a quarter of referrals in 1994–95 were for reasons such as recent bereavement, anxieties about being at university, academic English or stressful home circumstances.

When they contact the LDU, students are asked if they would like to undergo some initial screening. This involves completing a 'Yes/No' questionnaire on a range of difficulties and symptoms associated with dyslexia. They are asked to submit a piece of coursework, in different stages of completion if possible, and to do a piece of timed hand-written composition without help or using a dictionary. Staff encourage students to write about their own experiences of learning and the effects of their difficulties. Although this is quite demanding, almost all students return the materials. This screening material is used as the basis of subsequent meetings with students to discuss their concerns and to establish a course of action. If appropriate, students are asked if they would like to be formally assessed for dyslexia.

For most students, this formal assessment is essential for accessing support, through the DSA, for technology, tuition or personal helpers, and for them to be allowed alternative examination arrangements at the university. The LDU employs one psychologist on a part-time basis to administer assessments as well as several external psychologists on an individual contract basis. Contractual psychologists are given an induction to the university, its services, and given guidelines on conducting assessments, writing reports and making recommendations for support within HE. They are also kept apprised of technology developments and given demonstrations or practice in technology recommended by the LDU. Most assessments made for UEL students take a 'curriculum-based' approach, identifying the type and frequency of errors the students make and the strategies they currently use for reading, spelling, writing, speaking, remembering, organization, and working out time and direction. Typically, psychologists supplement this by psychological tests such as the WAIS-R (Wechsler Adult Intelligence Scale – Revised), WAIS memory tests or Ravens Progressive Matrices depending on the circumstances. Local Education Authorities (LEAs) administer the DSA and some will not accept a dyslexia assessment which does not include the WAIS-R. UEL issues guidelines to the psychologists it employs for assessment. For example, although the results of sub-tests of the WAIS-R can be illuminating, it is not considered appropriate to include an overall 'IQ' score, or to quote such scores to students. Similarly, reading or spelling ages are not included in the assessments as they are not helpful in considering support strategies, and can cause a great deal of distress, however well they have been explained.

It is most important that students themselves want to undergo assessment. They may need prior reassurance about what it entails, as well as post-assessment counselling. Students respond very differently to a diagnosis of dyslexia, although it is common to experience immediate relief that there is an explanation for their difficulties and that there are people who take them seriously. This is usually followed, at some point, by a series of emotions, ranging from anger at parents and teachers, anxiety about their abilities to overcome their difficulties or to succeed at university, self-criticism about their attitudes to similar symptoms in their own children, and confusion about which parts of their lives and personalities may or may not be affected by their dyslexic experiences. For example, one student with co-ordination difficulties wondered whether the nausea he experienced whenever he brushed his teeth was due to his 'dyslexia'.

WHAT KIND OF SUPPORT IS AVAILABLE TO DYSLEXIC STUDENTS AT UEL?

Policy and infrastructure

It is important to emphasize that dyslexia support operates within a wider infrastructure of support for student learning, and in an ethos of consideration for students who would not traditionally have entered most universities. UEL operates an equal opportunities policy; this policy, the UEL Mission Statement and its Student Charter all explicitly refer to the needs of students with disabilities and the desire to widen access to a greater range of students. New academic staff are required to take a post-graduate certificate in teaching and learning which includes dyslexia-awareness training. Additionally central services such as the library and individual subject areas have organized staff-development, or invited dyslexia staff into course team meetings to discuss particular issues. UEL events such as the annual Admission Tutor Forum, include a consideration of some aspect of dyslexia or disability. All staff receive the *Diagnostic Pack*, a copy of the *Skills for Success Guide* given to all students and *Tutor Notes to the Skills Guide*, which together outline ways of identifying and assisting students with a range of needs. Increasingly, departments are offering study skills units and subject-specific support materials to help students to orientate to the study requirements of HE.

Despite these efforts, students are still wary of declaring dyslexia, or indeed, anything which can appear to be a 'problem', for fear that this will be held against them either at Admissions, when their work is being assessed, when selecting subject options, or when they request job references. Anti-discrimination policy is very important in offering some reassurance. However, students fear any loopholes which may exist, particularly with respect to unseen references.

Publicizing services

Publicity about services is important not only to communicate what is available, but to reduce feelings of isolation and to encourage people to claim what help may be available. UEL issues a *Disability Handbook* to students. There are also leaflets aimed at prospective students giving pre-admission advice, or aimed at current students advertising the service, particular events or workshops. The library, Student Union, student services and departmental secretaries also help to disseminate information, for example, by setting up dyslexia noticeboards in their areas. Induction events for new dyslexic students appear on the official induction week timetable. The Student Dyslexia Society, supported by the Student Union and the LDU, has a stall at Freshers' Fair, and organizes its own events and newsletter.

General services offered to dyslexic students

All students assessed as dyslexic are offered services which include a formal needs assessment. This makes recommendations for technology; personal helpers (such as readers, scribes, proof-readers, technology training, one-to-one study skills support, or speech therapy); alternative examination arrangements, and on ways that teaching staff could help. Each student is given an information pack and handbook, which includes guidelines on how to access the different types of support available, as well as general information about dyslexia, study skills, and external organizations. Students applying for the DSA are offered assistance in applying to their LEA: the administrator checks that suppliers' pro-forma match the psychologists' recommendations, checks for obvious anomalies and puts the claims for different services together. Workshops which look at study skills from a dyslexic perspective are offered as well as some individual study support. There are also drop-in surgeries twice a week for general enquiries.

UEL has, so far, made a commitment to offering free dyslexia screening and assessment of dyslexia. This has proved to be very important as, on the one hand, those seeking alternative examination arrangements usually need to present formal documentation of disability to examination boards, while on the other hand, access to technology and personal helpers, financed through the DSA, is usually on the basis of an accepted formal diagnosis. As most UEL students are unlikely to be able to afford to pay for their own assessment, dyslexia provision would be discriminatory if access to free assessment were not made available. However, expertise and tests to assess overseas students for whom English is a recent language are not always available. This is an issue which is difficult to resolve.

Study support

It has to be emphasized that students, once diagnosed, are not put on to any kind of 'remedial' programme regarded as applicable to all. For many students, the lack of appropriate assistance over a lifetime means that they will not be able to tackle all of their difficulties while also studying for a degree. In practice, it is difficult for students to find time for even one hour a week with a support tutor. Instead, students negotiate with their tutor a programme of support based, in part, on their dyslexia assessment or needs assessment. However, they also have to prioritize areas for support on the basis of the subject they are studying. For example, science students may need to focus on strategies for exact, close reading of texts, discriminating between similar words such as 'ethane' and 'ethene' and writing sequentially. For subjects such as cultural studies, strategies for reading in bulk, for widening vocabulary, understanding esoteric styles, and producing more elaborate language structures may be more important. Subject disciplines vary in requirements for writing style and technical accuracy, the emphasis placed on grammar, and preferences for active or passive voice. Individual course assignments raise particular issues: for example, essays, reports and case studies require different structures, layout, planning strategies and writing styles. In addition, the students themselves are more prepared to tackle some areas of difficulty than others, either because they have strategies on which they can build or inhibitory emotional responses based on previous negative experiences. There are in-built conflicts, sometimes, between skills the student must develop, the work they have to produce by a certain date in order to stay on a course, and their emotional or physical limits at that time.

The following case studies illustrate differences in both the types of difficulties which students experience, and the kind of support 'package' which they required. They also indicate how different aspects of the service might integrate.

CASE STUDIES

Chiara: the role of on-course support

Chiara returned to formal education, via an Access course, after a twenty-year gap in her formal education. She saw a leaflet about dyslexia support when she attended an open day at UEL and came along to the unit to discuss her needs before application. The FE course where she was taking her Access course had recognized that she had severe writing difficulties but they had not the resources to finance a dyslexia assessment or more than limited language support, and Chiara could not afford to pay for these herself.

The LDU arranged for Chiara to be assessed soon after the first semester began. A diagnostic dictation revealed a spelling error rate of forty per cent, with many letter reversals and several unrecognizable words. She also was given half an hour to write about herself, which showed that she was able to write quickly and at length, but with such inaccuracies in grammar, punctuation and spelling that her writing, although neat, was impossible to read. Her own reading consisted of slow decoding and imaginative guesswork. However, she was able to recognize correct spellings quite well from a spell-checker. Among other things, it was recommended that she use a word-processing package with spellchecker and a synthetic voice facility, *Texthelp!*, to read her work back to her from the screen. She had also found it hard, on her Access course, to make notes in lectures as the effort to recall any spelling at all for some words interrupted her listening. It was suggested that she use a tape-recorder to supplement her notes. Chiara was very confident about her oral abilities, her mathematical skills, and her aptitude for anything practical.

It took three months for Chiara's claim to the LEA to be processed and the recommended technology to arrive. In the meantime, her first piece of work, handwritten, was submitted. Her lecturer, astounded at the disparity between her written work and her excellent seminar work, asked the LDU to organize a training session about dyslexia for all departmental staff. Subsequently, lecturers approached Chiara, offering assistance, moral support and encouragement. One of Chiara's difficulties with the course was in accessing new vocabulary both from reading and lectures; some lecturers provided her with glossaries so that she could match the meaning and spelling of subject specific vocabulary. When she described her difficulties in lectures, they also offered her copies of their lecture notes. Chiara noticed that the notes were word-processed and asked if she could have them on disc, so that she could use the synthetic voice on her computer to read them back to her, which was agreed by some lecturers. Chiara uses her own notes and her tape recording of the lecture to compensate for the computer's sometimes bizarre pronunciations.

Using her technology and working at her own pace over very long hours, Chiara was able to achieve some of the highest marks for course and project work. However, she was very anxious about working under timed conditions where she could not re-work her answers. She had never previously passed any examination, except for Maths. It was agreed that she should word-process her exam answers, and be given additional time to complete her answers. This added to her confidence as it reduced her panic, gave her time to structure her answers which she found difficult to do, and to proof-read and spell-check her work to some extent. The LDU gave Chiara a certificate to attach to her work, alerting markers to her particular difficulties and offering guidance on how to mark her answers. Chiara also attended workshops on revision and exam techniques. With her dyslexia support tutor, she developed strategies for analysing questions and structuring answers. It became clear to her tutor that Chiara's reading of exam questions was too inexact – her reading was so slow that, faced with a list of questions, she read only the key words and tried to guess what the question was. It was agreed that in the short-term, somebody would read questions to her in the exam. In the event, the tutor who read the questions found that he needed to alter stress and intonation in order for the questions to make sense. Despite these alternative arrangements, Chiara found it difficult to write examination scripts of a high standard. In some exams she did well, but she passed others only after a re-sit. Her overall marks, when averaged out, were still high, but an alternative to timed examinations might give a fairer assessment of her abilities.

Annette: a support package for reading difficulties

Annette's difficulties were recognized early by her parents who, though not educated themselves beyond the age of fourteen, sat with her every night from childhood, encouraging her reading, and searching for words in the dictionary. She is very articulate, and the final versions of her written work are of an extremely high standard. Writing tasks take her a long time to complete, not least because she has some difficulties finding and ordering words when writing.

However, Annette's greatest difficulties are with reading. She has Meares-Irlen syndrome (Irlen, 1991), which can occur with or without the pattern of other dyslexic difficulties. Because of this, Annette is unable to read for more than a few minutes before the text begins to blur, move, flicker and glow. Letters and words change place. She cannot always tell where one word ends and the next begins. As she reads, the text becomes increasingly mobile; it is hard to keep looking at the page, and she experiences nausea, headaches and frustration. All of her life she had thought that other people experienced text in the same way – but that they were better at coping. Despite a widespread acknowledgement that students with such difficulties cannot work for more than a short period at a time, Annette argues that she cannot let extreme discomfort prevent her from studying as all study tasks take her so long. She usually studies for eighty hours a week, even in the holidays, aiming for a first class degree.

Annette finds pink tinted papers and glasses with pink lens help to stabilize the text when reading, and to reduce glare. However, the text is still mobile and blurred. As large print is easier for her to read, she makes enlarged tinted photocopies of reading material. With a support tutor, she looked at reading strategies to make more effective use of her reading time. Because her slow decoding meant she often forgot what she had already decoded, she was trained to use visual strategies to help to anchor words and ideas in her memory. Unfortunately, not all reading material is amenable to easy visualization. She also tried highlighting so she could find keywords easily, and writing summaries in the margin to reduce the need to re-read whole passages.

Nonetheless, as the reading demands of the course rose, Annette began to fall behind. Her friends were all commissioned to put text on to tape. Her LEA agreed to pay for her to have up to twenty hours of material put on to tape every week. Annette also started to use the *Arkenstone* machine for the partially sighted but she could only use this when on campus. Instead, she purchased a scanner so that she could scan good-quality texts into her computer, and then use the synthetic voice facility to read the texts aloud. Once scanned into the computer, the text could also be altered: the colour of the screen and text changed, the font changed, the font enlarged, and the whole page put into double spacing. It was also discovered that some texts similar to those Annette needed for her course were available through the National Listening Library.

A combination of strategies, readers and technology have enabled Annette to access information more easily. Library staff have helped by reading titles from catalogues, extending loan deadlines, finding books, and allowing Annette to take home books to try out on her scanner. However, even though Annette works long hours, she has had to extend her course over an additional year. Her LEA have agreed to extend her grant because of her specific difficulties. Annette mentions that the personal and emotional costs of study have been great. Because her work is of such a high standard, she finds that some students, and even staff, question whether her difficulties are real.

Kiran: individual support for organizational skills

Kiran reports a typical dyslexic pattern of development and displays many reading and writing symptoms associated with dyslexia, although in a very mild form. However, he has great difficulties with physical co-ordination, time, direction and general organization. He failed his first year, mostly because of failing to find exam rooms or turning up on the wrong day. During the year he had missed lectures and seminars because of confusing dates; he missed deadlines for assignments; he lost notes and irritated his tutors. He lost four electronic organizers. His friends describe him as being like a 'mad professor'. Over the last year, Kiran's support tutor encouraged him to talk through how each difficulty arises in the course of a day, and to think through strategies for himself. For example, he needed not only to purchase and keep a diary, but to develop a colour and place coding system for diary entries, a regular morning regime so that he remembered to check the diary, strategies for confirming the day and date, and routines for putting the diary in the same place. He has developed a mental map of the campus by using landmarks, and walking out routes he needs to use until he is confident about them. Kiran also benefited from talking through organizational strategies with other students, particularly on planning backwards from deadlines. Kiran is an interesting case in that his difficulties are not primarily language based and are not evident through typical curriculum-based assessment; nonetheless, he is one of very few 'dyslexic' students at UEL who has had to retake a year.

Selina: technology support

Selina's reading difficulties were very similar to Annette's and a similar package was recommended. However, Selina was very anxious about the technology. She continually called out the suppliers or rang the IBM helpline, thinking the technology was defective or broken, until they refused to help any more. Although she attended word-processing workshops at the university, she was too anxious to take in what was said, and too embarrassed to admit that there was something else which she found difficult.

However, a support tutor realized that Selina had added numerous spelling errors to her user dictionary so that it was no longer reliable. She suggested that Selina ask for additional individual technology support, which was arranged by the LDU, using DSA funding. It was discovered that, like many students who had purchased equipment through the DSA, Selina did not know how to perform even the most basic functions such as naming files or formatting discs. She could not make sense of manuals or on-screen instructions. She did not know how to use the voice facility and, even if she had, it could not be used to read on-screen directions. Her tutor focused, at first, on building her confidence and on developing brief, visually based worksheets on separate functions such as using a tool-bar or changing font size. Selina made rapid progress: her technology tutor referred to her as 'a quick learner'. However, many students mention that they become aware too late of the range of uses to which their technology can be put, and ways in which they could have combined the different pieces of technology to develop new strategies.

STRENGTHS AND LIMITATIONS

The case studies above provide examples of students who received support packages geared to individual needs. Thanks primarily to HEFCE funding of projects and use of the DSA, additional staff were employed to offer necessary assistance. This has allowed many students the support they needed not only to succeed as students, but to achieve good degrees, and to proceed to excellent careers.

Unfortunately, the picture for some students is less rosy. The increasing numbers of dyslexic students strain existing university support resources, so that students are increasingly reliant on the DSA to fund their support. However, LEAs vary greatly in how they administer the DSA, in what they regard as evidence of difficulty, in the type of technology or personal helper support they will finance, and on the amount of money they will release to each student. Some LEAs will support a student application for three thousand pounds worth of technology, but not support the technology tuition which would ensure its use. It is impossible to offer any guarantees to students about the level, range or timing of support they will receive through DSA. Students usually have to begin courses without knowing if they will have the support they need to succeed. They are also caught up in disputes over where responsibility lies for funding their support (the university or the DSA) and challenged on whether their difficulties are real. Moreover, part-time students are not eligible for the DSA. Sometimes this pressurizes those with most difficulties, and who might benefit from studying part-time, into full-time study.

The allocation of all disability funding to individual students means that it is difficult for universities to develop an infrastructure for support. As more dyslexic students are attracted to universities already offering support, it becomes difficult for those universities to maintain current levels of support for any individual student. Universities who employed a tutor to support a small number of students, and offered any examination provisions that were necessary, find they are faced with enormous difficulties when the numbers of students presenting with such difficulties multiplies by several times each year.

Existing support tutors activities can become re-directed into making assessments of need or assistance in making DSA claims. Universities with large numbers of dyslexic students need additional financial support to enable support to be effectively in place from pre-application onwards. Alternatively, more pre-application facilities need to be provided by LEAs to enable assessment of needs and support packages to be in place for the beginning of semester for previously assessed students, and interim support arrangements for those undergoing assessment. Current arrangements mean that the LDU cannot plan a support package for any student until funds have been agreed, which can be many months into a student's course. It also means a reliance on hourly paid tutors, who may need to find alternative employment while waiting for funds to be agreed.

UEL is currently trying to address some of these issues, for example, through a pilot scheme in making dyslexia-useful technology available in computer centres. *Texthelp!* has been provided on the computer network, and soundcards available in a pilot lab. Technology worksheets and some technology workshops and surgeries have been provided for dyslexic students from the beginning of the first semester. This means students have a greater chance of accessing technology before their DSA claims are processed, and it offers some facilities to overseas and part-time students. Dyslexia workshops offer some general, though limited support for new students, and gives students opportunities to share strategies.

FUTURES

It is likely that the immediate future will be dominated by funding issues, and university dyslexia services, nation-wide, will be shaped by financial contingencies rather than student requirement. However, it is clear that there are still new areas of support which need to be developed for dyslexic students. For example, it seems likely that pre-enrolment requirements are likely to increase. In 1995, twenty prospective students approached the LDU for pre-course interviews, assessments of their needs for technology and personal support, and information about the university and its support. There were no such enquiries two years ago. Applicants also requested demonstrations of equipment, and help with applying for equipment for the DSA – resource intensive activities when there is no guarantee that those students would attend UEL. Nonetheless, it is understandable that students should want to prepare their claims before they start their courses, in order to receive technology and support from the commencement of their courses. It is also apparent that students want to know much more about the type of reception and support they will receive from course staff, which puts additional pressures on Admissions tutors. It is likely that UEL services will have to alter in some way to accommodate rising pre-entry enquiries.

Students have said they would prefer to have a key-worker to oversee the different aspects of their support package, which is something we will look into. There are also other difficulties associated with the scale of support now offered. For example, when there were only four known dyslexic students, it was relatively easy to arrange for sheltered accommodation for examinations and to find an invigilator. When there are three hundred students needing separate rooms, invigilators, readers, scribes, proof-readers, examination arrangements can become a major operation, especially if rooms with natural lighting and without background distracting noises and disability trained personnel are required. Some course tutors are faced with ten students who all require different examination arrangements. The unit is looking into ways of supporting departments in offering a range of alternative examination arrangements. The aim is to reduce the likelihood of decisions about alternative arrangements being made on grounds of restricted sources. It is hoped that this support would reduce pressure on course staff, ensure greater equity, enable adequate briefing for invigilators, and reassure students that there are people on hand who understand their needs.

HEFCE financing of Dyslexia Projects in Universities (1993–95) saw many universities starting what they thought was a small service, only to find themselves overwhelmed by numbers and by the range of requirement. This has meant services have had to develop very quickly or very hard decisions have had to be made about where to allocate meagre resources. Many services are waiting to see, on the one hand, where the numbers will settle and, on the other hand, what resources will be available. In such unstable conditions, it is hard to set priorities, to plan ahead, or to discuss how 'entitlement' can be defined for dyslexic students in an HE context.

However, it is to be hoped that, over the next five years, some of these issues will be resolved and that the focus will shift to monitoring outcomes and setting quality standards.

REFERENCES

Ellis, D. (1984) *Reading, Writing and Dyslexia: A Cognitive Analysis*. London: Erlbaum.

Irlen, H. (1991) *Reading by the Colours*. New York: Avery.

Miles, T.R. and Miles E. (1990) *Dyslexia: A Hundred Years On*. Milton Keynes: Open University Press.

Pumfrey, P.D. and Reason, R. (1991) *Specific Learning Difficulties (Dyslexia): Challenges and Responses*. London: NFER-Routledge.

Stein, J.F. (1994) A visual defect in dyslexics? In A. Fawcett and R. Nicolson (eds) *Dyslexia in Children: Multidisciplinary Perspectives*. Hemel Hempstead: Harvester Wheatsheaf.

Thomson, M. (1984) *Developmental Dyslexia*. London: Whurr.

5

Extending the role of the co-ordinator for disabled students

Lea Myers and Viv Parker

> It needs ingenuity and a strong taste for battle if all those who would benefit from education after school are to be enabled to enjoy it. (Warnock, 1995, p.51))

INTRODUCTION

Nationally, the equal opportunities agenda has been well established for some years. Many HE institutions now feature a commitment to equal opportunities on their mission statements and the University of East London (UEL) was one of the first to introduce an equal opportunities policy. During the early 1990s, however, it was not uncommon for the discourse of equal opportunities to omit all reference to disability. Just two examples of this were the Royal Society of Arts report (Ball, 1990) and the Open University television programme (1990) on widening access to Higher Education. One of the difficulties for HE institutions committed to equal opportunities is that participation rates of students with disabilities are difficult to establish. Nevertheless, our enquiries lead us to believe that there is still much work to be done in the HE sector to enable all students to participate fully.

Disabled students are likely to encounter several different kinds of barrier to their full participation in higher education. These are physical barriers in the form of inaccessible buildings and facilities; financial barriers such as the lack of funding for special equipment and personal support needed to enable them to study; negative attitudes such as the belief of tutors and others that, for example, a blind or deaf student will require more staff time than the institution can afford or provide; and ignorance and inflexibility such as that displayed by a tutor who told one of the authors of this chapter that a blind student cannot study French as it is taught in a 'very visual manner'. A more difficult barrier to identify and remove may be that which results from completely overlooking, omitting or being unaware of the needs and capacities of people with disabilities.

The two main issues that need to be addressed to promote disability equality are: to ensure that there is an explicit policy statement and commitment to its promotion, and that there are the necessary strategies, systems, resources and other steps taken to make the policy a practical reality. At the University of East London (UEL) we decided to start with policy and use that as a means of encouraging more students to come to UEL to study.

This chapter aims to identify and discuss some strategies for making HE more 'user friendly' to people with disabilities. It will do this by drawing on some case studies at various levels of provision. The first is at national level, in particular the Disability Discrimination legislation; the second is at the sector level, the Higher Education Funding Council for England (HEFCE) initiatives; the third is at institutional level based on UEL and will include individual case studies of students. We aim to identify the main barriers that prevent or impede the entry of disabled students to HE, and how these might be reduced or removed. This material will be discussed and analysed to explore some of the means by which policies on equal opportunities may be made more inclusive and some methods whereby the policy or mission may be implemented. One particular strategy that will be discussed is the role and value of a designated member of staff to develop and co-ordinate services for students with disabilities.

In this chapter we refer to special needs, disabled students and students with disabilities. We think it as well to comment upon this terminology. We are aware that 'definitions ... are powerful' (Tomlinson, 1995, p.7) and that the language of disability is therefore contentious. For example, the term special needs, although adopted by Warnock as a move away from the medical model is 'now perceived by many as simplistic, pejorative and patronising'. (ibid.) Nevertheless, it is still commonly used by professionals (Hewitson-Ratcliffe, 1995, p.9) and, we think, reflects the nature of further and higher education, which is not yet inclusive. That is, the current educational environment and context is discriminatory. If it were not there would be no 'special' needs. Similarly, we have discussed whether it is more acceptable to describe students as having disabilities, as in 'students with disabilities', or as 'disabled students'. We have considered the arguments of various disability organizations for their preferred terminology and recognize that this is no mere semantic point but a matter of politics. We have used the terms interchangeably as we believe that they are not mutually exclusive. We think it also important to note that the Department for Education and Employment invites university applicants to indicate the nature of their disability on the University and Colleges Admissions Service (UCAS) form. Categories of impairment are used, and these will influence the ways in which people respond. For example, different categorization systems elicit different responses from different populations with different requirements. Finally, we would stress that impairment does not always present a learning problem and that where it does this can, generally, be overcome.

THE NATIONAL CONTEXT

Legislation to protect people with disabilities from discrimination in a way comparable to that offered to women by the Equal Opportunities Commission, and members of different ethnic groups by the Commission for Racial Equality, is closer than it has ever been. The Disability Discrimination Act (DDA) received Royal Assent on 8 November 1995 (*Disability Now*, Dec. 1995, p.1). Its effects on education are more limited than the organizations campaigning for full civil rights for disabled people have pressed for, one reason being that 'education provision is still excluded from the main provisions of the Act which outlaw discrimination' (*Skill Newsletter*, issue 28, p.1). The Act does, however, place a new statutory duty on HEFCs to 'have regard to the requirements of disabled persons' and HE institutions will be required to publish disability statements outlining their provision (ibid.).

The HEFCE has set up a disability advisory group to advise it on disability issues, and the HEFCE now has a statutory duty to require institutions to produce a disability policy statement. Brian Fender, the Chief Executive of the Council, identified two purposes of these statements: they are to inform prospective students of the nature of provision within individual institutions and to inform Council and Government of the nature and extent of provision across the sector (Fender, 1995, p.7). This requirement should significantly prompt institutions towards the introduction and development of their policies towards disabled students. Policy statements are easier to influence than improvements to provision, as the latter has resource implications. Professor Fender has indicated that the HEFCE will have to consider 'ways of targeting its resources' (p.6) and that institutions will have to contribute funding from their own resources (see Chapter 10 by Cooper and Corlett).

In distributing formula capital funding, there has been a reluctance by the HEFCE to in any way direct the use of this funding or to do more than encourage 'institutions to consider the needs of students with learning difficulties or disabilities in determining the use of these funds' (DFEE, July 1995, p.19). However, the HEFCE special initiative funding offered in 1993–94 and 1994–95 across the sector to promote access to HE for students with disabilities and learning difficulties has very 'significantly raised the profile of disability' and progressed the policy and provision for students with disabilities in many institutions (op. cit., p.5). The special initiative funding was made available to institutions of HE with a proven track record of implementing work with students with disabilities who were invited to bid for funds to carry out research leading to the development of best practice. At UEL we were fortunate to be awarded substantial amounts in both years. One outcome of the work has been an awareness of the value of the named person or co-ordinator for students with special needs/disabilities.

As long ago as 1978, the committee headed by Mary Warnock (1978, p.9) recommended that, 'higher education establishments should publicise their policy on the admission of disabled students and make systematic efforts to look after their needs.' At that time, Warnock pointed out the need for a single 'named person' to support disabled people through the bewildering and confusing array of services and professionals with whom they would be required to negotiate. The need for such a role in FE colleges is now well documented (Corbett and Barton, 1992) but is less widely acknowledged at diploma and degree level (see also Chapter 1 by Sheila Wolfendale). Writing more recently, Warnock again highlighted the need for a named person in HE by pointing to some of the additional difficulties experienced by disabled students (1995, p.51):

> If they can find a place on a course that will suit them, will they or will they not get a grant from their education authority? Can they get to the course? Where can they get special equipment, if they need it? Is there anywhere suitable for them to live, if they need to be away from home? The answers to these questions, and many more, have to be sought in numbers of different places, and the answers of the different agencies involved may contradict each other.

Warnock has focused on those difficulties experienced at entry or pre-entry. However, disabled students continue to be faced with barriers on course, and on completion or exit. A number of countries, including Germany, France, Sweden and the US 'require their higher education establishments to appoint a contact person' (Van Acker, 1995, p.9) and, in the UK, this measure has been advocated by Skill (National Bureau for Students with Disabilities) as an important component of an effective policy and practice at HE level. Nevertheless, the extent to which it has been adopted by institutions in the UK appears to be limited.

The 1995 Guide to Higher Education for People with Disabilities (Skill/Hobsons, 1994) contains a listing of 174 entries by HE institutions. Of these, only 47 mention a named person or contact with some responsibility for special needs/disability. Eighty-eight identify as the contact an institutional role (with or without a name) with no obvious connection with disability, e.g. Assistant Registrar, Secretary; and, for 47, the entry consists solely of the institutional name and address.

A survey undertaken for the RNIB in 1992–93, although focusing on provision for students with 'significant visual impairment' (Patton, 1993, p.1) also asked more general questions about the institutional provision for students with special needs/disabilities. Responses were secured from 111 colleges of HE (a response rate of 69.4 per cent) of which 62 had a named person with responsibility for special needs, two had an additional adviser for visual impairment, and 29 had no adviser available. While this appears to demonstrate a commitment to disabled students, it should be noted that half the named advisers had no time allocation, and only seven had a full-time allocation to undertake the duties of the role (Table 5.1).

Table 5.1 *Time available to advisers* (Patton, 1993)

Time	Number of advisers
No special time allowance	30
Less than ten hours per week	23
11–20 hours per week	7
Full timetable	7
Question not answered	5

The value of the role, and the effectiveness of the person who occupies it, will depend upon the resources allocated to support it. One key resource is time and, as Table 5.1 indicates, this is generally restricted. Patton also found that only five advisers had received any formal training in any aspect of special needs (1993, p.4). It is apparent that many institutions have developed only a limited appreciation of the need for a named person as support co-ordinator for disabled students, and of the tasks associated with the role.

KEY COMPONENTS OF CO-ORDINATOR ROLE

The Scottish Higher Education Funding Council (SHEFC), set up at the same time as the HEFCE, as its first step in attracting more disabled students, initiated an audit of all HE institutions, the results of which were published in January 1995. This was followed up by asking universities how they would like to see funding in this area targeted in the future.

Their response was that they would like to have a member of staff in each institution with a specific remit for guidance and support for students with disabilities/special needs, and also for staff. Accordingly, institutions were invited to apply for matched funding for such a post, which the majority did. Paul Brown (1995, p.23) the National Co-ordinator, who facilitates the post holders in their work explains:

> Almost all Scottish institutions have co-ordinators/advisors for students with disabilities/special needs, many are implementing or updating policies and re-assessing procedures, all have new equipment for students and prospective students and most importantly all, without exception, are seriously looking to improve their provision and support for students with disabilities/special needs.

The work done at each institution is not prescribed by the National Co-ordinator, but inevitably his support will ensure that all institutions benefit from the work of the others, 'in order to improve the general situation for students' (p.24). In this context a variety of approaches to the role may be advantageous. There has not been the same degree of cross-over of practice in England.

In July 1994, Viv Parker undertook a survey of the members of the Skill South East Region Group (Parker, 1995) in order to establish the nature and extent of the service offered to disabled students, and to explore the factors which affect applications and entry to higher education. Forty-two questionnaires were distributed to staff with some responsibility and/or interest in working with students with special needs/disabilities. Of these, 16 were returned (38 per cent response).

Twenty-two different areas or issues were named as being covered by the institutional policies, although only two of the institutions had a policy covering all of these. The most commonly shared areas of policy were admissions, examinations, access, and equal opportunities. The exact nature of the post and its responsibilties were seen to vary considerably between institutions. In part, this is possibly connected to the time allocation. Nevertheless, this would not account for the variation in location of the post holder. For example, of the 16 responses the majority (10) had a named person located in Student Services. The others were either in an academic department (one in education, one in engineering) or some other form of central service, e.g. Education Development Service, Secretaries Office, and Estates were specified. It was unclear exactly how the location may be deemed to affect the nature of the role, although it was significant that only 56 per cent of the respondents indicated that advice and support for students with disabilities was one of their main responsibilities, and only 50 per cent had an input to policy making. Whether the items not specified, for example, liaison with LEAs, recruitment, staff development, and so on were the responsibility of another member of staff in the institution cannot be inferred from the responses. Nevertheless, the data does indicate that, in approximately 50 per cent of cases, the role of co-ordinator is severely restricted in terms of the support offered to disabled students.

DEVELOPMENT OF SERVICE FOR STUDENTS WITH DISABILITIES AND SPECIAL NEEDS AT UEL

Most initiatives require a 'driver'. When the initiative is in some way externally required or forced upon an institution, perhaps such as that arising from the Quality Assurance/Audit process, that institution will quickly appoint staff and allocate resources to review and develop current policy and provision. Initiatives without such backing may have little or no institutionally funded support and rely on volunteers to 'drive' them. This is how policy for disabled students developed initially at UEL. In the absence of any data about the numbers of students with disabilities at the university, it was difficult to argue for services for them:

> It was a bit difficult because we didn't have a policy and we didn't have any students with disabilities as far as we knew, so from the management point of view there wasn't any point in putting a resource in because they didn't know whether there was really a need. And because we didn't have a resource or a policy we couldn't publicise or do anything, so it was a sort of Catch-22. (Viv Parker in discussion with Lea Myers, July 1995)

However, at the time referred to (1989–90) the institution had a Dean of Equal Opportunities and an equal opportunities committee with a special needs and disabilities sub-committee. The sub-committee was co-ordinated by one of the authors of this chapter, Viv Parker. The first tasks identified by the sub-committee were to encourage more students to apply to the university and to offer more effective support to those who came. A meeting was arranged during 1990 for representatives and interested persons from all institutions and organizations used by people with disabilities in the local area to advise us on strategies. One major strategy identified was the need for colleges, schools and other organizations to be able to make contact with a named person at the university to deal with enquiries on behalf of students. This meeting provided the first network of contacts at local institutions and has been extremely useful for two-way information and contacts between the university and its feeder institutions.

At this point the subcommittee co-ordinator, with the support of the committee members, worked entirely on a volunteer basis to develop the university policy and service with four main aims:

1. to publicize the Disabled Student Allowance (DSA) to all students and potential applicants
2. to develop a positive policy on admissions, on-course support and examinations
3. to identify and offer guidance and support to individual students
4. to collect data on students with disabilities and their experiences.

The attainment of these aims was aided by a number of factors: the introduction in 1990 of the DSA, the establishment of University policy; and winning a bid for funds from the university's Enterprise Unit.

Publicity for the DSA

From an institutional perspective, one major concern about making an explicit commitment to encouraging more students with disabilities into HE is the fear that it will be very costly to the institution. One reason for this is the general stereotype of the disabled person as a wheelchair user who will require ramps and lifts to be installed across all sites. This is an inaccurate image as only a very small percentage of disabled people are wheelchair users, and while it would be desirable to have these facilities it is not necessary to exclude disabled students because they are not yet in place. In addition, an important national development which served to counter this fear was the introduction of the three DSAs in 1991/92. These are funded centrally but administered via the student's LEA. They are available to full-time students who are eligible for mandatory awards for study to meet any 'extra costs on their course because they are disabled ... to enable them to benefit fully from their courses' (DfEE, Nov. 1995, p.1) and are subject to means testing. For 1995–96 the rates of the DSA are

- up to £4,850 per year for non-medical personal helpers
- up to £3,650 for the whole course for equipment
- up to £1215 per year towards general disability-related expenses.

The introduction of these allowances seemed at the time, in the absence of any institutional commitment of resources, to offer all the funding a student would need to study in HE. Internal publicity of the allowances helped allay the concerns of university management that this would be a costly initiative, and encouraged students to identify themselves to the university co-ordinator, thereby making the documentation of need possible. Externally publicising them served to encourage potential applicants and their advisers to see HE as a viable option, and to make contact with the co-ordinator, again facilitating data collection. Information on the DSA was put in newsletters to staff and students, and is now in the prospectus, pre-enrolment pack, and regularly in staff and students' newsletters.

Establishment of university policy

The priority was to draft, and submit for approval, a policy document in relation to disabled students. The policy recommendations were drawn from various Skill publications and included three areas: admissions procedures, supporting students on course, and modification for exams and assessment. The stated aim of the policy was to make the university an enabling and barrier-free educational environment rather than an obstacle course. The recommendations were brought before academic board and, with the support of the Dean of Equal Opportunities, approved on 19 September 1990.

Although the policy was established there were no additional resources available to support it. The recommendations, that a named person would be available as a contact for potential students and for arrangements for assessment and examination modification, were not possible to implement without the designation of someone to this role. Again, this presented problems since it was necessary initially to establish the need for such a person. One valuable initiative which highlighted the need for this appointment was a drop-in for students with specific learning difficulties (dyslexia). This was set up by Sheila Wolfendale from the Psychology Department, and the student response established the need for the service. (See Chapter 1 by Sheila Wolfendale, and Chapter 4 by Stella ni Ghallchoir Cottrell for a more detailed discussion of dyslexic support.) Another key factor which helped to establish the service for support for students with disabilities and learning difficulties was winning a bid for funds from the university's Enterprise Unit.

Availability of enterprise funding

The Enterprise Unit funding was used to:

- audio tape the prospectus
- conduct a survey of disabled student opinion and experience
- produce a staff development video on disability
- investigate, in collaboration with the charity Workable (Voluntary Sector Consortium Promoting Employment of Disabled People), the transition from college to work for students with disabilities.

The audio tape of the prospectus made the information available to blind and dyslexic students and emphasized the university's commitment to supporting disabled students.

The survey was based on a questionnaire sent to all those students (122) who, at the point of enrolment in 1991, had indicated that they had a disability or special need. It was designed to find out what their requirements were for support at UEL, and the extent to which these had been met. Fifty-three responses were received (43 per cent). Most of the special needs indicated were not such as to require extensive modification of facilities, course material or assessment arrangements, nor did they require a high level of special support. Some disabilities were 'invisible' and largely controlled, such as asthma, diabetes and epilepsy. The responses indicated a low level of information among the students about sources of support of all kinds, and most said that they would value better information, guidance or counselling. Respondents reported positive experiences of studying, including receiving help and support from staff and other students, but there were some less favourable responses which gave cause for concern. For example, one student reported being required to 'prove' a disability in front of others. Such an incident demonstrates a lack of awareness about what constitutes disability, as well as insensitivity on the part of staff.

The student survey emphasized the need for an active policy supported by someone with responsibility for ensuring its imple-

mentation and development. The need for increased staff awareness of the requirements of disabled students, and of their
attitudes to disability was demonstrated to be a crucial step in the
development of a whole college approach to support. Staff development in a large university is by no means easy because staff
rarely come together. One solution was to produce a video which
could be used by each department at its own convenience, and
even by individual members of staff. The video was made with the
help of students who had responded to the survey. They spoke
about and demonstrated the barriers they faced at university, such
as inflexible methods of teaching and assessment, lack of staff
awareness, and inaccessible facilities. A key message of the video
was that small changes in practice would make a significant difference to the learning experience of disabled students, and would
benefit all students. Funding made it possible to distribute free
copies of the video across the HE sector.

THE CO-ORDINATOR'S ROLE

As Viv Parker, the co-ordinator of these initiatives was also a full-
time lecturer, the time available for the service was very limited.
As the various initiatives became increasingly effective, and the
number of students at UEL and applications for places increased,
the need for a time allocation for the role became greater. There
was now hard evidence of the need for the service. During the
academic year 1994–95 over 100 applicants to the university
'ticked the box' on their UCAS form to indicate a disability; 289
students 'ticked the box' at enrolment, and all of these were
contacted in writing and offered information about services.
Approximately 130 new students made personal contact over the
year for advice and/or support and, of these, 70 had not previously indicated a disability. What these figures mean in the context
of the co-ordinator's role can be illustrated by two recent case
studies. The names of the students have been changed but, in
every other respect, they are factual.

Sue: mobility and personal support

Sue has recently come from the local FE college to study at UEL.
She uses a wheelchair for mobility and needs academic and
personal support plus special equipment to study effectively. Her
first contact with UEL was at pre-application stage, when she tele-
phoned to discuss her needs and how UEL might meet them. This

was followed by an informal visit to the campus, where the co-ordinator showed her around the site and they discussed the facilities. There was an in-depth conversation about all aspects of university study and of the personal support and/or equipment that Sue might need to enable her to study effectively. This resulted in Sue putting in her application, through the UCAS system, to study at UEL.

Following the application, the co-ordinator had telephone discussions with Sue's care staff and her social worker. She then arranged a meeting at the university, between herself and Sue, Sue's support worker, her social worker, and two tutors from the Higher National Diploma (HND) course which had made Sue an offer of a place. The discussion identified the fact that the extensive group work involved in the HND might require many hours of personal support and that the locations chosen for the group meetings, which could be off campus, would possibly present difficulties. Course tutors resolved to approach the Business Studies staff about reconsidering Sue's application to the degree course, which involved less group work and which had been her first choice. Sue was offered, and accepted, a place on the Business Studies degree course as a result of this.

The co-ordinator then entered into further discussion with Sue, her social worker and support worker, about her personal support and equipment needs, in order to identify specific support requirements. For example, when would Sue need a note-taker, and for how long? When would she require library or lecture based support? What personal care support would be required? And which sources of funding – LEA or Social Services – would be appropriate to each? Also identified were Sue's equipment needs and her travel requirements. A detailed report of all these needs, and the justification for every item, was written and copies sent to LEA and Social Services with requests to each for funding for the appropriate elements. Quotes for equipment were obtained from suppliers and these too were sent with the request for funding. This was followed with various telephone discussions with all staff at the university, with Sue's social worker and support worker, and with the LEA and Social Services.

Agreement from the LEA to fund a note-taker and library support and equipment was, in this case, given quite quickly. Unfortunately, this was the first time personal support had been requested in this manner from the Social Services, and they did not have a procedure to agree it. As a result, and because it was not possible to identify the staff to take on the support roles until funding was fully agreed, the co-ordinator had to follow up the request to Social Services periodically over the summer vacation. Advertisements for people interested in taking on the support work had been drafted and publicized on campus and at the local job centre.

Just two weeks prior to the start of term Social Services agreed to fund the hours requested. It then became necessary to contact those who had responded to the advertisements to see who was available, suitable, and acceptable to Sue. Next, the transport arrangements had to be checked, and equipment ordered. This involved more telephone calls to the appropriate services, to suppliers, and to Sue and her family.

Once a personal support worker was found for Sue, and the new academic term had begun, a meeting was arranged between the support worker, Sue and the co-ordinator to agree the terms of employment, payment, and procedures etc. Sue is officially employing and paying the helper for the LEA funded portion of the work, i.e. notetaking and library work (about 12 hours weekly), and the Social Services is employing and paying the helper directly for the personal care element, i.e. pushing the wheelchair/access to toilet and other facilities. This is quite complicated to arrange and monitor, so several meetings were needed for clarification.

Sue's needs in relation to assessment and examination were a further area for discussion, and resulted in formal requests to tutors for amendments, e.g. extra time and separate accommodation. Sue's request for information about the emergency evacuation procedures highlighted considerable gaps in university provision, which involved the co-ordinator in discussion with the Health and Safety officer. These discussions are still ongoing, and involve exploration of the procedures and equipment used at other universities. Another area of university provision highlighted by Sue and her support worker was the lack of sanitary disposal bins in the toilets which were recently refurbished for disabled students. This required the co-ordinator to contact the bursar, who suggested a temporary solution to which she agreed.

Sue's wheelchair was old and unsuitable for her use but she had no funds to replace it. Staff from her previous college offered to undertake fund-raising for her to purchase a more suitable model and they sought university support. Discussion of this took several hours of co-ordinator time during which a suitable system which did not stigmatize or identify the student was discussed. It also became apparent that the university needed a battery recharging facility on campus. The co-ordinator is currently undertaking investigations which she hopes will result in the identification of a suitable location and appropriate equipment.

Amin: communicator support

Amin is deaf. He first contacted the co-ordinator prior to entry to ask what communication support was possible. The co-ordinator contacted the LEA to ask for funding for communicator support, for their agreement to pay the university for the provision of this support, and for a PC/word-processor and minicom. Suppliers were contacted and quotes for suitable equipment secured. Agreement from the LEA was received just prior to the start of the course. By this time the City Lit (a further education and Community College in Central London) was unable to offer communicator support, and so the co-ordinator had to meet with the university finance and payroll departments to set up employment contracts and a special budget to enable the employment and payment of the communicators. Course tutors were contacted in order to establish Amin's timetable, and which sessions were priority for communicator cover. A number of communicators were then contacted and asked if they could offer support to cover the timetable. Eventually two people were offered contracts to cover the whole week.

As the funding would not cover all of his classes, meetings were arranged between Amin and the communicators, in order to agree which sessions were priority for support. At the start of the academic year, tutors were advised of the presence of a deaf student and his communicator. The accommodation officer was consulted about procedures for emergency alarms in the student hall of residence occupied by Amin. Some modification to the telephone arrangements were also required, given that there is just one pay phone in each hall of residence, and the loan of a minicom from registry was arranged until Amin's own machine arrived. Arrangements for examinations were discussed with tutors. Extensive delays in the provision of equipment which had been ordered for Amin's use, resulted in many phone calls to the supplier.

After all this had been dealt with, the main task undertaken by the co-ordinator was the arrangement and monitoring of communicator support and payments for it. As the university had never had such a budget before the payments were quite complicated and involved many meetings over timesheets and computer print-outs. Many contacts with the LEA were needed as they had paid some of the communicator funding directly to the student, although he had been unaware of this, and it was difficult for UEL to retrieve the money from him. There were also meetings over changes to timetables, absences of communicators, and additional sessions, all of which involved payment arrangements being altered and further discussions. The other matter which took some time was consultations with the Estate Services over a suitable visual alarm system for the halls of residence, and negotiations over sources of payment for the system. Securing quotations, getting the work completed and explorations with finance over the possibility of VAT exemption also took time. The final tasks involved were arrangements for communicator support at the degree award ceremony, i.e. who would do it and who would pay for it, and arrangements for similar support at job interviews.

These two case studies illustrate the level of support currently required by disabled students at one institution of HE, the importance of having one member of staff co-ordinating the support, and the amount of time required to undertake the duties associated with the role. As more disabled students enter HE it is to be assumed that as systems become more firmly established, and all staff have a greater awareness of how they can work to support a wide range of student needs the role of the coordinator in directly supporting students may reduce as other aspects of developing the service take precedence.

DEVELOPMENTS IN THE SERVICE AND THE CO-ORDINATOR ROLE: ANALYSIS AND DISCUSSION

The early emphasis of the service at UEL was on encouraging the entry and admission of students with disabilities. As the number of students entering increased, securing the personal equipment and support they needed within the classroom became the priority. At the same time, it has always been important to keep records of those applying, entering and seeking the support of the service since, without this, any case made for resources, policies and services would not be taken seriously. Another major role of the co-ordinator has been to monitor the experiences and concerns of students with disabilities at UEL. Each year a questionnaire has been sent to all students who have indicated a disability, whether they have been in personal contact or not. The responses have been very useful in identifying areas of the service which need improvement. We have become increasingly aware that to ensure that students with disabilities have the same quality of experience as other students requires improved access to all services across the whole institution. Many of these needs do not become apparent to an institution until the barriers to the admission and entry of students with disabilities have been largely removed. These things require monitoring and recording and information feeding back into the university system with recommendations for action. The needs identified are unlikely to be addressed unless there is at least one person with interest in, and responsibility for, the service and some budgetary provision.

A quality service involves access to all the extra curricular activities, student support services, and learning support across the institution and this will involve some institutional investment. Over the last two years Access funds and HEFCE funding has been an invaluable source for improvements to infrastructure and other costs. These are very important in the short term but, as the evaluation of the HEFCE special initiatives indicated 'funding with a one-year time-scale limits the longer-term development of improvements' and this 'suggests that a future approach should adopt a longer-term funding initiative ... and ... place much greater emphasis on a commitment to assimilating an activity by the institution involved' (Fender, 1995, p.6). Ideally this should be the next goal of a service for students with disabilities, that the institution fully assimilates it, along with all other equal opportunities initiatives, into all mainstream service provision.

The chairman of the Quality Enhancement Advisory Group states (Roberts, 1995, p.iii):

> It is widely acknowledged that guidance and learner support is becoming increasingly important for all students, particularly as it contributes to the maintenance of academic standards and the quality of the student experience, and ultimately the performance of the institution.

The document 'aims to give institutions an advisory framework which may be appropriate when they are considering the quality of guidance and learner support arrangements'. We feel it can be adopted to provide a comprehensive framework for guidance and support including disabled students. These guidelines identify four phases of learning, and present the main guidance and support activities required for each. Adoption of these guidelines as part of a quality control mechanism would, we feel, contribute to the development of a whole institution approach to learner support. Nevertheless, as the number of disabled students coming to UEL increases, and more of those coming have more complex support requirements, the co-ordinator's role is unlikely to become redundant in the short term.

CONCLUSION

The commitment to a policy of equal opportunities was easier to realize when it was a matter of the university meeting the needs of the 25 students with known special needs in 1991. At UEL, we now have about 400 students with disabilities. Their requirements are substantially greater, their expectations increased and staff goodwill is no longer sufficient as the resource for meeting these. Improved services at FE level are enabling more students to qualify for entry to HE. The high profile debate and lobbying which has accompanied the various attempts to secure Disability Discrimination legislation has contributed to raising the expectations of disabled people. The potential and actual demand for HE is likely to increase substantially. Experience tells us that the barriers to full participation can be reduced or removed.

We have used the term co-ordinator to cover a wide range of different tasks. At the institutional level, the role includes developing a whole institution service for students with disabilities, and the development of learning support policies and systems. However, the role also includes supporting individual students with disabilities to enable them to access the facilities, finances and equipment necessary to study effectively, i.e. 'learner' support. Adopting a continuum approach to support requires the review and development of all services supportive to learning. Ideally this should substantially reduce the need for 'special' support with the exception perhaps of students with more extensive and multiple impairments. If institutions do focus on supporting learning across a wider range of student needs then many students with disabilities will be supported effectively as part of that provision. However, as services at school and FE level improve and students with more extensive impairments and multiple disabilities seek to enter HE, the need for a co-ordinator to facilitate their entry and studies will continue. This is a function not only of the needs of those entering HE but of changes in the structure and resourcing of HE.

As institutions develop semesterized and modularized modes of curriculum delivery, the pressures on students in HE increase, as does their need for support and guidance. As resourcing of HE is reduced the mainstream sources of support for students becomes increasingly stretched, hence the need for 'special' support for some students seems likely to continue. The co-ordinator must ensure that a balance is kept between providing the essential personal support that many students with disabilities need, and developing the service across the institution. The aim is to ensure

that the institution 'owns' the service and sustains a commitment
to its continuation regardless of the particular person in post.

REFERENCES

Ball, C. (1990) *More Means Different: Widening Access to HE*, RSA Final
Report. London: Department of Employment Training Agency/RSA.
Brown, P. (1995) A degree of change: advances in provision for students
with disabilities/special needs in the Scottish higher education sector.
Skill Journal, 52, July, 21–4.
Corbett, J. and Barton, L. (1992) *A Struggle for Choice: Students with Special
Needs in Transition to Adulthood*. London: Routledge.
Department for Education and Employment (1995) *Further and Higher
Education Review Programme, Disability Discrimination Bill, Interim Report*.
London: DFEE.
Disability Now (1995) Finally, it's law!, *Disability Now*, December p.1.
Fender, B. (1995) Good practice in higher education. *Skill Journal*, 53,
November, 3–7.
Hewitson-Ratcliffe, C. (1995) The development of learning support in
post-compulsory education. Unpublished PhD thesis, University of
East London.
Higher Education Quality Council (1995) *A Quality Assurance Framework
for Guidance and Learner Support in Higher Education: The Guidelines*.
London: HEQC.
Open University (1990) *Widening Access to Higher Education*. Television
programme: *Open Forum* 19 July.
Parker, V. (1995) The role of the co-ordinator for Students with Special
Needs in HE. *Skill Journal*, 53, November, 15–21.
Patton, B. (1993) *RNIB Support Service Provision in Higher Education*.
London: RNIB.
Roberts, G.G., (1995) *A quality assurance framework for guidance and learner
support in higher education: the guidelines*. London: HEQC.
Skill (1994) *Higher Education and Disability: The 1995 Guide to Higher Educa-
tion for People with Disabilities*. Cambridge: Hobsons.
Tomlinson, J. (1995) Disability, learning difficulties and further education:
the work of the FEFC's specialist committee. In C. Hewitson-Ratcliffe
(ed.) *Current Developments in Further Education: The Third John Baillie
Memorial Conference*. London: Skill.
Van Acker, M. (1995) Higher education for disabled students: not there yet
but on the way. *Helioscope Quarterly*, 3, (Spring) 23–4.
Warnock, M. (1978) *Meeting Special Educational Needs: A Brief Guide to the
Report of the Committee of Enquiry into Education of Handicapped Children
and Young People*. London: HMSO.
Warnock, M. (1995) The Warnock Report: 1995 perspective. *Skill Journal*,
52, July, 50–2.

Responding to consumer needs: working towards a quality service

Jenny Corbett and Jean McGinty

> *Unfortunately, most worthwhile educational objectives, and particularly those dependent on institutional change, take so long to achieve that in practice evaluations tend to be of intermediate objectives which rarely capture the complete effects of the change.* (Elton, 1995, p.152)

We begin our chapter with this quotation because it encapsulates the dilemma faced by evaluators such as ourselves. We were invited by the Project Director and Special Needs Co-ordinator, Viv Parker, to evaluate the ways in which aims and objectives had been addressed and to reflect upon any potential difficulties which might influence further developments. As a combined team of internal (Jenny Corbett) and external (Jean McGinty) assessors, we were able to both monitor the institution against its past history and compare it to the national context. The educational objectives set by the initiators of learning support systems at the University of East London (UEL) were far-reaching and ambitious. Inevitably, therefore, they will take time and sustained effort to achieve. It seems important to us that we recognize, from the outset, that we are placed in a position where we are evaluating intermediate objectives and can only speculate upon the long-term outcomes.

In relation to the developments at UEL, we will evaluate current services and policy, reflect upon the impacts and effects of the Higher Education Funding Council England (HEFCE) initiative and make recommendations for a quality model. This specific case study will be set in the context of current changes and challenges in HE in Britain and the rest of Europe. It is important to ask the following questions.

- To what extent does the growth of learning support provisions at UEL reflect overall changes in the HE sector?
- How do the characteristic features of UEL as an institution influence its receptivity to initiating this growth?

- What quality indicators should be employed to indicate 'fitness for purpose'?

When using terms like 'consumer needs' and 'quality service' it is essential to clarify just who our consumers are, what they say they need and how 'quality' can be defined in relation to the institutional mission.

THE CHALLENGE OF CHANGE IN HE

Throughout Europe, the ancient traditions of a liberal and autonomous university education are being challenged. In the German context, Butzer (1995) refers to the atrophy of universities to becoming mere providers of services. Mass Higher Education in Germany has fostered a degree of anonymity and lack of respect (Butzer, 1995, pp.9–10):

> Ten thousand students have become the norm. The social recognition earlier associated with the status of student has been lost. The buildings are capacious, functional, and anonymous, with no cosy corners. In the German mass universities conduct such as vandalism, of a kind that is never encountered in private environments – writing on walls, disrespectful actions such as stealing books, tearing pages out of books, or keeping borrowed books past the due date – are the order of the day.

In France, Bireaud (1995) suggests that the traditional pedagogical model is now outdated and that new missions in the universities have led to the introduction of such models as 'pedagogy by objectives' whereby 'the knowledge and know-how to be acquired are defined in terms of behavioural objectives and criteria of evaluation based on observable performance' (p.33).

Teichler and Kehm (1995) stress that graduates are now competing for more marketable skills and need to accumulate several of these to be attractive to employers, while Saunders (1995) recognizes the difficulty of measuring the value of work-based skills.

Before we focus upon Britain, in particular and on disability and learning needs specifically, it is necessary to reflect on these broad changes which have long-term economic and political implications. Learning support systems in British HE are symptomatic of much wider changes in European universities. Mass HE has brought in a new clientele, with significant implications for pedagogy and expected outcomes. The ways in which the old models functioned are no longer suitable for the demands placed upon them by the new learners and altered conditions of educational resources. It is important to recognize, as Armstrong (1995) emphasizes, that European countries do not produce homogeneous definitions and concepts of what constitutes a disability or a learning need, yet it seems imperative that we take a European perspective upon this issue and avoid isolating it as a peculiarly British dilemma.

Undoubtedly, the impact of mass HE in Britain is changing the system and its practices. The Higher Education Quality Council (HEQC) has been concerned to devise minimum 'threshold' standards. As Kingston (1995, p.2) says:

> Top of the long list of issues which gave rise to the projects were the rapid growth in the numbers of students registered in UK HE institutions – 65 per cent between 1990–91 and 1994–95 and the doubling in numbers of degree-awarding institutions over the same period, from 50 to almost 100.

This expansion and its resulting impact led the HEQC to conclude that the wide range of students – both school-leavers and mature – now going into universities precluded setting standards at the input end and on-course.

If we are exploring the extent to which the growth of learning support provision at UEL reflects overall changes in the HE sector, we need to acknowledge the following major influences:

- a culture of individualism and institutional anonymity;
- a pedagogy of behavioural objectives and observable performance;
- an emphasis upon transferable skills;
- a wide variation of academic standards on entry to the university sector.

We will now examine the characteristic features of a 'new' university, of which UEL is a typical example, for it is in the new universities that learning support has been so enthusiastically embraced.

'IT IS OUR MISSION': RESPONDING TO CONSUMER NEEDS

Mass HE has significant implications for all teaching staff in the 1992 universities. A 'science don' was recently quoted as saying that in his new university most of the 30 students a year on his course needed extensive 'nursemaiding'. He said, 'I would say that maybe 60 or 70 per cent of them, perhaps more, are really struggling' (quoted in *Guardian Education*, 1995). The rhetoric of 'learner autonomy', so prevalent in current university parlance, assumes that the learner can take a major responsibility for the management of learning programmes. As Hodkinson (1995, p.9) suggests:

> The current relentless obsession with a crude form of individualism ignores models of education based on collegiality, risks blaming the victim for any inadequacies and failures of the education system and provides no effective way of addressing the deep seated inequalities in British Higher Education.

If, as the 'science don' implies, many of the students are seeking help in order to cope with the demands of their courses, the availablility of learning support is crucial. Yet, the inequalities of the British HE system are such that the old universities are relieved of so pressing a demand to respond to consumer needs while the new universities are overwhelmed with pressure for services.

A sure indicator of this academic inequality is the emphasis upon 'transferable skills' within the new university sector, where specific subject areas assume less significance. Anne Francis, as head of the Careers Advice Service at the University of East London, says, 'They are looking for skills appropriate to any workplace – teamwork, communication and organisational skills': (p.4). In this context, the learner is held responsible for acquiring a range of social and life skills, nebulous in nature.

It is against this background that we examine UEL as a case study. Earlier chapters in this book have indicated how well established are the learning support structures and valuing of prior learning experience for students coming to the university. This service was fully operational before the HEFCE special initiative enabled this university, along with 29 others, to extend and consolidate its learning support provision, with specific reference to the needs of students with learning difficulties and/or disabilities. It is important to recognize that this baseline of awareness of need and provision of services existed. In our evaluation, we will reflect upon the ways in which current services have been further developed and new initiatives created through the HEFCE funding. We will then set this case study into the context of the national special initiative and reflect on how it compares with other similar universities.

In the current climate, responding to consumer needs is inextricably bound up with performance indicators, accountability and enhancement (Yorke, 1995). Our evaluation will explore the performance indicators to assess quality provision which it seems appropriate to apply to UEL. We will assess 'fitness for purpose', taking into account the mission of the university and its student intake. In its 1996–97 prospectus, UEL states that its mission is 'to provide the highest possible quality of education, training, research and consultancy, in order to meet the needs of individuals and of the communities and enterprises in our region'.

This emphasis upon a local and regional community is significant in terms of learning support, for the university serves a locality in which the take-up of HE is traditionally exceptionally low. This makes the role of a learning support service all the more important, in relation to a 'quality' provision.

EVALUATING THE OUTCOMES OF THE HEFCE INITIATIVE

We will evaluate the outcomes of the HEFCE project in three stages:

1. as it applies to UEL;
2. as it relates to the national special initiative projects;
3. within the context of quality assurance in HE.

These stages form the substance of our sequential analysis: the first stage is to look inwards at the case study institution; the second stage is to set it against other comparable institutions; the third stage is to measure special needs initiatives within a general focus upon quality assurance in HE. In this framework, we are operating as traditional researchers who need to contextualize and generalize case study examples. We also demonstrate our divergent perspectives, of internal and external evaluator, to move from the particular to the general.

The project at UEL

UEL has been funded by the HEFCE for two years from 1993–94 (£95,000) and 1994–95 (£85,000). As the provision for students with learning difficulties and/or disabilities was already well established, through equal opportunities developments and the creation of a Study Skill Drop-In Centre (see Chapter 1 by Sheila Wolfendale), this formed a robust baseline from which to extend services. The university took the bold step, in the first year of the HEFCE initiative, to address a broad and diverse range of issues, including developing learning support for curricular access, improving site access and information and developing careers services. It was moving towards a whole institutional policy in which overall provision needed to be addressed. We reflected that, while admirable in its scope, this broad-based initiative is extremely demanding and onerous for the small team of specialist learning support staff working with the co-ordinator for special needs. Our observation (Corbett and McGinty, 1994, pp.3–4) was:

> We recognise the present transitional phase in which specialists are endeavouring to improve the skill of all staff, releasing them to concentrate on complex needs and development issues. From our interview data we noted that a high proportion of students with specific learning difficulties only received this diagnosis on entry to the university. Diagnosis has become a demanding and time-consuming element of learning support with significant implications for resourcing.

Both of these key issues – the responsibility being asked of mainstream teaching and administrative staff and the demands of diagnosing students with specific learning difficulties (dyslexia) – are central to our stage three analysis of quality assurance in HE.

The second year of the HEFCE initiative was designed to consolidate the development of that first year by establishing a learning support service provision, assisting students with specific learning difficulties (dyslexia) with computer technology and evaluating transition planning from further into higher education. The employment of staff on short-term contracts has enabled administrative services to be considerably extended and rationalized, so that the co-ordinator can spend more time on national networking, staff development and related research activities (see Chapter 5 by Myers and Parker). However, it has all the limitations of short-term funding, involving lengthy periods of staff initiation into what is inevitably a complex and bureaucratically labyrinthine institutional maze, whereby staff are no sooner becoming used to procedures than they see their contracts ending. This involves the co-ordinator in time-consuming management issues which detract from the benefits of additional staffing resources. We observed (Corbett and McGinty, 1995, p.5) that:

> Whilst it is important to address specific short-term needs, it is also essential to focus upon the establishment of good practice across the whole institution. The lack of time allocated to managers tends to drive them towards crisis management rather than a pro-active, reflective and well planned model.

This difficulty in being able to address long-term planning to ensure continuity and strategic development was a particular cause for concern. We considered that the implications for institutional policy embedding were significant.

> At the time of writing this report, there was no firm evidence of an institutional commitment to the continuation of core staffing for the support service. There are a lack of systems which ensure that this developing area of work is built into strategic and forward planning, although well-documented recommendations have been made. This leads to a lack of confidence that resource allocations will be forthcoming to support long-term planning and development. The good track record of the institution has resulted in an increasing number of applications from students needing a range of additional support. This could lead to an overload on one institution with other institutions avoiding an involvement in what is inevitably a high-resource activity. (p.7)

This uncertain situation has significantly changed. A management commitment has been voiced throughout the HEFCE project, as this extract from the *Times Higher Education Supplement* of 26 August 1994 (p.6) confirms:

> Last June, Frank Gould vice-chancellor of the University of East London, confided off the record: 'Even if the funding council won't fund our work on disabilities, we'll get the money from somewhere – but I don't want that publicised just yet.'
>
> His statement demonstrated the university's commitment to students with disabilities, but fortunately Professor Gould was saved the fund-raising headache.

At this stage, the second year of HEFCE funding was forthcoming and the project was externally supported. After the two-year period of external funding, the senior management at the university has supported the appointments of a full-time administrator on a two-year contract and a support tutor for students with specific learning difficulties on a two-year contract, thus assisting a continuing of provision.

The national special initiative projects

It seems to us that we cannot evaluate the impact of this initiative upon one specific institution without reflecting on the national response (see Chapter 10 by Cooper and Corlett). The HEFCE Report, published in January 1995, is most valuable in this respect because it offers an evaluation of the general issues and themes which emerged from an analysis of all the projects. The report noted the following three common factors: the need to be realistic when setting objectives and scope; collaboration in all its forms is shown to enhance the potential of a project; and funding is a key issue, particularly the short-term nature of this initiative.

We will discuss each as they relate to the particular case study example which we evaluated.

The need to be realistic

In our case study, the original objectives were very ambitious and led to a considerable work over-load. The scope was then more focused for the second year but the demands of the project were still overwhelming.

Collaboration

There was active collaboration, in our study, in which networking and joint initiatives (like the production of a video) developed knowledge, skills and liaison pathways. The personnel involved in our case study university are now acknowledged nationally as valuable practitioners in this developing area and are being contacted by less experienced staff in other institutions.

Funding

The danger of a pump-priming exercise is that the long-term embedding in institutional policy is dependent upon the level of management commitment. Our case study illustrates the dilemma faced by specialist staff when they are left uncertain as to how the work is to be sustained and what mechanisms they can realistically establish. While, in this example, a continuity of provision has been ensured by a supportive senior management, the degree of insecurity which such a situation generates is hardly conducive to confident, clear planning and embedding.

The HEFCE is philosophical about the variation in management practices across the range of projects. The report (HEFCE, 1995, p. 17) states:

> With the support of their institutions, some projects have thought creatively about future finance and have made arrangements which will enable the work started to continue or to extend its coverage. But many other projects have received less support from their institution and have been forced to see their work come to an end at the close of the funding period. It is likely, however, that many of the policies they developed or the work they started will be continued. In the long term, any action which has raised the profile of disabled issues even for a short period, will contribute to the overall raising of the baseline for future work in the field.

Within the context of this approach, our case study has undoubtedly demonstrated an increased disability awareness and a response to student needs which has fundamentally influenced the culture of the institution.

Quality assurance

Quality assurance has to relate to fitness for purpose. In some universities, this will mean ensuring a high level of scholarship and opportunities for student research; in others, the emphasis will be on teaching and learning at undergraduate level. If we recognize that there are distinctive differences within British HE and that addressing consumer needs at Oxbridge will, therefore, require a particular set of procedures while addressing consumer needs at UEL will require another, we can begin to assess what constitutes 'fitness for purpose'. When a new university like UEL encourages non-traditional students to apply, it has to establish systems to ensure that they do not fail. As Ainley (1994) noted, in his comparative research on a 'home counties' university and an 'inner city' university, placing learners in a situation where many of them will fail or 'drop-out' early in their courses does them no favours at all. It, therefore, becomes the duty of any new university like UEL to develop effective learning support systems. We recognize that the HEFCE initiative at UEL was to provide improved services for students with learning difficulties and/or disabilities but, as the details of this provision have already been documented earlier (in Chapter 4 by Cottrell and in Chapter 5 by Myers and Parker), we will focus on two specific aspects: staff development and consumer demands

These seem to us to be the two sides of the coin of quality assurance, in that the demands require changes in practice and changes in practice lead to new demands.

Staff development

As more and more students have come forward to seek learning support in the form of additional tutorials, classroom support, study skills training and exam arrangements, the need to prioritize has become essential. The small team of specialist staff have to concentrate their energies on those with the greatest need. Unless more mainstream staff across the institution agree to share responsibility for learners with specific needs, which may mean a considerable modification of their habitual teaching practice, the capacity to cope is threatened.

It is interesting to us, both coming from a background in FE that recent research supports a Further Education Funding Council (FEFC) model in HE. In relation to quality assurance, Hustler (1995) notes that:

> Poor performance or high drop-out rates now cost the institution itself; here, first-rate, pre-entry guidance and on-course guidance represent important preventative mechanisms (see, e.g. FEFC's 'Funding Learning'). In short, if the HEFCE funding methodology shifts towards that of the FEFC, senior management might well prioritise the importance of guidance.

This transference of an effective model from one sector to another indicates how important it is to establish a baseline against which priorities and strategies can be identified (Fry, 1995; Middlehurst and Gordon, 1995). However such an adoption from the FE sector, while useful for quality audits, may seem sinister or threatening to an HE teaching staff already overwhelmed with the process of change.

Shore and Roberts (1995, p.13) suggest that an emphasis on 'total quality' in HE can serve to fuel discontent 'While management theory might hold that this has a beneficial effect (since the employee is goaded towards constant self-improvement), in reality, particularly in the context of HE, this situation results in fear, destructive internal rivalries and the fragmentation of solidarity'. The HE sector, in particular the new 1992 universities which often constitute an amalgamation of disparate smaller institutions, may be said already to characterize a fragmented solidarity before any external measures set one section in competition with another. In exploring barriers to change, Halsall (1995) suggests that the inclusion of guidance modules as a curriculum elective, while useful to many students, is likely to meet with resistance from some subject areas who prefer to see this initiative as the responsibility of central units like student services. What is becoming more apparent, in the current 'quality audit' climate, is that staff development is only likely to be effective if it is firmly located in a context of consumer demand and consequent institutional responsibility. In other words, it seems unrealistic to expect that a reliance upon equal opportunities policies in HE will be sufficient to change teaching practices, despite a recognition that these policies are contextually related and need regular reappraisal (Farish *et al.*, 1995).

Consumer demands

The changes in practice which the HEFCE initiative allowed – i.e. to improve, expand and advertise UEL's competence and confidence in supporting students with specific learning difficulties (dyslexia) and other related study skills problems – has greatly increased consumer demands. As Cottrell records in Chapter 4, the numbers of students coming forward for diagnosis and support have grown dramatically each year with significant implications for staff management and resourcing. To assess how this compares with other new universities, it is important to set the UEL situation into a national context. In a reflection on the special initiatives nationally, Bekhradnia (1995, p.4) said 'it would seem that all of the projects concerned with dyslexia support were totally overwhelmed and failed to correctly estimate the staff resources required for the project ... by and large projects seriously underestimated the extent of latent dyslexia among their students'.

Disregarding the controversial nature of dyslexia as a disability, as it would require a detail of discussion outside our brief, it is important to acknowledge that these consumers of services are now finding a definite voice. While the large group of learners in FE who are categorized as having learning disabilities rarely act as forceful advocates without staff support, this particular group in HE tend to be effective self-advocates. The long-term implications of serving the needs of students with specific learning difficulties (dyslexia) in HE have to be addressed within the context of accountability and enhancement.

In the language of school improvements and school effectiveness, a key research area in current educational projects, it is essential to assess the 'value-added' element if a new university is to be evaluated against its 'fitness for purpose'. As in the school context, there is a struggle between competing objectives. Schools are expected to meet targets in the academic league tables while at the same time having to address the specific needs of their population. This can result in their being criticized for what is a valiant effort to be fit for their purpose. The new universities are now expected to join the highly competitive and unequal competition for research rating while at the same time trying to meet consumer demands. If they encourage too high a proportion of students who require support services, will this be rewarded with a 'remedial university' status and low standing in the research community? It is a contradictory element of quality assurance, be it in school, further or higher education, that what is a quality response at one level can become a quality deficiency at another. There are ethical issues which either pull an institution back towards its mission or allow it to break free into a cut-throat and ever-changing market.

CONCLUDING REFLECTIONS

We now reflect on some of the dilemmas which can arise in evaluating consumer needs in a quality service, and offer some recommendations for a quality model. Our approach in this chapter has deliberately been to set our case study into a much broader context and, in so doing, draw upon the views and perceptions of a wide range of researchers and practitioners. However, in our final recommendations we use our own experience of the evaluation and our interest in post-16 provision, policy and practices relating to learning difficulty and/or disability. In this respect, we are presenting our views for critical appraisal by colleagues and are hoping to open up some issues for further debate.

The gradual erosion of the traditional university pedagogy and the inclusion of 'quality assurance' measures can risk replacing an excess of conservation with a new conformity (Pratt, 1995). The development of new guidance modules and support systems threatens to relocate the privileged position of mainstream HE and to redefine its relationship with the margins (McNamee, 1995). If the learner support structures are to become embedded in university practice, mainstream lecturers need to be convinced that 'Learning to Learn' courses are developmental rather than remedial (Norton and Crowley, 1995). Harker (1995) explores the concept of quality in HE, using a postmodern analysis. This is useful in relation to the learner support and 'special needs' emphasis because it opens up new ways of seeing old forms and, in the process allows for changing perceptions. If, as this analysis implies, it is the cost of financing equity and increasing access which has resulted in the recasting of the value of a modern university in performance and economic measures, it suggests that innovation arises through accident. Harker reflects (1995, p.38) that 'occasionally, the traditional emancipating role of higher education converges with social policy and this results in significant equity and access benefits'.

It seems important to recognize that responding to consumer needs, in the case of students with disabilities and specific learning needs, is more at the whim of governmental flux than derived as a result of strategic planning. Wedell (1995), in his reflective look to a future special education, suggests that gearing the system to learner diversity can be directly related to quality audits and effectiveness. When we speculate as to the level of inclusiveness which a future HE system can accommodate, it is important to stay open to the full range of potential consumers including those whose learning disabilities are more severe than are commonly found in British universities at present; (see, for example Parker and Corbett, 1991). Thus, a quality service needs to be ever adaptable to new and unexpected consumer demands.

Our recommendations for a model that includes policy, management and staff development are:

Policy

- A confirmation and embedding of student rights in all central government policies
- A coherent approach in all government departments
- Clearer guidance to the implementation of policies by local authorities and organizations to ensure a consistency of interpretation of government policy
- A recognition of the need established by pump-priming funding through a possible core and margin funding system
- A system to encourage longer-term planning and development as well as institutional stability
- The inclusion of learning support systems in HEQC inspections and as part of this process, to set learning support provision within the context of systematic internal and external audit and reviews
  These developments would encourage more universities to develop learning support systems, thereby creating a more equal opportunity for prospective students.
- A recognition by national research bodies of the need to promote research in this area of work, especially projects which monitor and evaluate the effectiveness of this newly developing initiative
  The growth of research data will encourage the sharing of information and insights to foster debate. Longitudinal studies will be of particular value in evaluating effectiveness.

Institutional management

- A commitment from senior management, and in their use of management strategies, to ensure provision is firmly embedded in both the mission statement and strategic and development planning

This is likely to result in a fairer equitable allocation of resources.
- The embedding of quality assurance and staff development programmes to support the work
- Clear statements from managements as to where responsibility lies for each area of learning support for both academic and support staff
- The establishment of clear lines of communications both to and from grassroots staff through the various tiers of management
- The setting up of task groups with clear objectives to offer an opportunity for the debate of current issues and the consideration and recommendations of future developments
- An analysis of the tasks necessary in offering a quality learning support service to be undertaken, and the allocation of these tasks to maximize staff skills and minimize expenditure
  This would avoid the continuation of a misuse of teaching staff time and the effective use of administrators.

Consumer needs

- Accurate, honest and positive publicity, clearly targeted and available in a range of media
  This should state the broad range of facilities available to students with learning difficulties and/or disabilities and how the university can respond to identified need.
- A receptive, welcoming approach including preliminary visits, enquiries and consumer assessment
- Thorough and appropriate systems of assessment at both pre-entry and entry which identify student support needs and offer a realistic response to clarify the level of support currently available
- The availability of counselling and guidance facilities to respond to individual differences
- An analysis of need in relation to the use of technology along with ongoing maintenance and re-assessment
- The availability of specialist facilities and trained staff in libraries and resource centres
- A national modular system which allows for credit accumulation over a flexible time span, and which is, therefore, more accommodating for students with disabilities
- A careers counselling and guidance service which is accessible throughout a student's university experience, and continues to support them into the early stages of employment

- Flexible arrangements for those requiring extra time or special facilities to carry out coursework and examinations, negotiated early in the course

Staff developments

- Staff training, needed by all staff if a whole institutional response to students' needs is to be established
- Additional, sustained staff development opportunities for specialist staff, with a major responsibility
- Staff development linked to strategic planning and including access to in-house and external programmes as appropriate
- Opportunities for staff networking and establishment of close, working relationships with external agencies offering specialist support, e.g. RNIB, SKILL
- Knowledge and understanding of the establishments from which students come

  Good transition planning can only take place when there is close liaison. When this is neither practical nor possible, the university needs some pre-preparation programmes to compensate for this lack of planning.
- Internal staff development programmes to facilitate understanding across departments of learning support processes
- Encouraging examples of good practice by sharing experience across the institution
- A recognition of the responsibility of specialists with an appropriate allocation of time and senior posts, thus according the work status and the creation of opportunities for promotion

Readers familiar with further education will recognize the similarity between these recommendations and those applying to that sector. They are made on the basis of experience of evaluation in an HE institution as well as experience in similar situations in FE. It is not our intention to lift these wholesale from one sector to another but to recognize the commonality of some aspects and to build on the experience and success gained in another sector. In our experience, we have found no other models being promulgated but these may well develop as universities create a more sophisticated response to student need. Our concerns centre around the abilities of institutions to strike a proper balance between two sometimes opposing but potentially complementary aspects of their work, i.e. research and high quality teaching and learning.

If we are to avoid the 'growing mismatch between student needs and staff interests', which Professor Gould, the Vice-Chancellor of

UEL, recently highlighted (1995), staff development is critical. Improving learning support is not solely a disability issue but is about the recognition of a new and diverse student population. To become a competitive society in which all those seeking life-long learning can access a facility which meets their needs, requires a barrier-free learning environment with an adequate and appropriate learning support system in place. Then we can, with confidence, talk about equality of opportunity.

REFERENCES

Ainley, P. (1994) *Degrees of Difference: Higher Education in the 1990s.* London: Lawrence & Wishart.

Armstrong, F. (1995) Concepts of difference within European educational and vocational policy. Paper presented at the European Conference on Educational Research, Bath.

Bekhradnia, B. (1994) Speech to the Higher Education Funding Council England Special Initiative Final Dissemination Conference. *Educare* **S1**, 3–6.

Bireaud, A. (1995) Pedagogy and pedagogical methods in higher education, *European Education*, 26 (4), 18–40.

Butzer, H. (1995) Back to the old ways? The universities have atrophied to providers of services, *European Education*, **26**,(4), 6–11.

Corbett, J. and McGinty, J. (1994) Wider Access for Students with Special Needs. An Evaluation Report presented to the Higher Education Funding Council for England.

Corbett, J. and McGinty, J. (1995) HEFCE Project on the Outcome of the 1994–95 Special Initiative to Encourage Widening Participation. Evaluation report.

Elton, L. (1995) Enterprise in Higher Education: issues of evaluation, *Higher Education Quarterly*, **49** (2), 146–61.

Farish, M., McPake, J., Powney, J. and Weiner, G. (1995) *Equal Opportunities in Colleges and Universities: Towards Better Practices*. Buckingham: Open University Press.

Fry, J. (1995) Quality judgements and quality improvement, *Higher Education Quarterly*, **49** (1), 59–77.

Gould, F. (1995) Agenda. *Guardian Education*, 26 September, p.3.

Guardian Education (1995) One academic is certain that expansion has led to falling standards. 12 September, p.2.

Halsall, R. (1995) Guidance and learner autonomy: some barriers to change. Paper presented at the Higher Educational Research Conference, Bath.

Harker, B. (1995) Postmodernism and quality. *Quality in Higher Education*, **1** (1), 31–9.

HEFCE (1995) *Access to Higher Education: Students with Special Needs.* London: HEFCE.

Hodkinson, P. (1995) Learner autonomy in Higher Education: in defence of complexity and defence of complexity and diversity. Paper presented at the European Conference on Educational Research, Bath.

Hustler, D. (1995) Agenda for guidance and learner autonomy. Paper presented at The European Educational Research Conference, Bath.

Kingston, P. (1995) Degrees of difference. *Guardian Education*, 12 September, 2–3.

McNamee, P. (1995) Bridging gaps: an analysis of Access programmes for persons of disadvantaged backgrounds. *Innovations in Education and Training International*, **32** (2), 106–11.

Middlehurst, R. and Gordon, G. (1995) Leadership quality and institutional effectiveness. *Higher Education Quarterly*, **49** (3), 267–85.

Norton, L. and Crowley, C. (1995) Can students be helped to learn how to learn? An evaluation of an approach to learning programmes for first year degree students. *Higher Education* **29** (3), 307–28.

Parker, V. and Corbett, J. (1991) Students with learning difficulties at the Polytechnic of East London, Department of Education Studies: a Skill research project. *Educare*, **40**, 12–15.

Pratt, J. (1995) Editorial: The critical value of HE. *Higher Education Review*, **27** (1), 3–6.

Sanders, C. (1994) Pulling down the fences. *TES*, 26 August, p.4.

Saunders, M. (1995) The integrative principle: higher education and work-based learning in the UK. *European Journal of Education*, **30**,(2), 203–16.

Shore, C. and Roberts, S. (1995) Higher education and the panopticon paradigm: quality assessment and disciplinary technology. *Higher Education Review*, **27** (3), 8–17.

Skill (1995) *Projects Update: Easter 1995*. London: Skill.

Teichler, U. and Kehm, B. (1995) Towards a new understanding of the relationships between higher education and employment. *European Journal of Education*, **30** (2), 115–32.

Wedell, K. (1995) Making inclusive education ordinary. *British Journal of Special Education*, **22** (3), 100–104.

Yorke, M. (1995) Siamese twins? Performance indicators in the service of accountability and enhancement. *Quality in Higher Education*, **1** (1), 13–30.

Peer tutoring: a collaborative approach

Jenni Wallace

INTRODUCTION

This chapter is a description of a project that took an American peer tutoring programme (supplemental instruction) and adapted it to meet the needs of students in the UK. The term 'peer tutoring' is a system of instruction in which learners help each other and learn by teaching (Goodland, 1979, p.13). It is based on the premise that all learning is student-centred, and recognizes that with a continued reduction of the unit of resource it is easy to lose the centrality of the learner in the process of education. It also recognizes that the most effective learning environment is one where learning is an active process fully involving the learner, preferably in groups in a supportive and non-threatening environment, and can be strengthened by a truly collaborative approach with student and tutor. Evidence shows that students increasingly feel that they are not supported in a mass higher education system and, with the changing nature of the student intake, there is a greater than ever need for a supportive learning environment. It is all too easy for busy and stressed academic staff to blame learners for their difficulties and deficiencies .

I have used supplemental instruction (SI) as one methodology to provide a framework to tackle some of the problems posed above. In particular SI provided a structured and active learning environment that supported the academic staff but did not drain staff resources, in particular staff time. The key to the success of the programme was effective awareness raising for academic staff, the training of the student leaders and the effective management of the scheme.

SETTING THE CONTEXT

USA

SI was developed in the US in 1975 at the University of Missouri-Kansas City (UMKC). SI was first offered to the health science professional schools, and was then extended throughout the institution. After a rigorous review process in 1981, the SI programme became one of the few post-secondary programmes to be designated by the US Department of Education as an 'Exemplary Educational Programme'. The National Diffusion Network (the national dissemination agency for the Department of Education) provided federal funds for dissemination of SI throughout the US.

UK

In 1990, Kingston University, along with other universities, was looking at the issues of maintaining quality while managing greater numbers of students with a lower unit of cash (Barnett, 1992). This project, along with others was adapted and developed for use in the UK. The successful outcomes of this work were such that, in 1994, the work was supported by a Higher Education Funding Council for England (HEFCE) grant that provided the funding for a consortium of universities to realize those adaptations and to develop the appropriate resources for dissemination nationally. The most significant difference that has been made in the UK is that the work is carried out in partnership with academic staff; it has an educational and staff development role which has considerable influence on changing the nature of an institution gearing itself to meeting learners' needs.

The three key factors of the American work identified as transferable to the UK

It was realized by the learning support group at UMKC that the traditional way of supporting learners having difficulties with their taught courses was very resource intensive (often one-to-one) and there seemed to be no conclusive evidence that this approach of separating course content away from the skills needed to effect learning was successful. A programme was developed then to integrate learning strategies into course content. The second major concern was to support an initiative that combated the increased attrition rate of first-year students, and the idea of using second-year students in a peer support way was realized. The second-year student, who still had a clear memory of how his or her first year had been, could act as a role model, sharing the strategies they had used to help with the survival skills needed to complete a course of study.

Third, and what I considered to be the most valuable aspect of the work, was the approach by the original group to change the following statement

> If students fail they have only themselves to blame, and must take the responsibility themselves.

into

> If you recognize that there are such things as **difficult courses**, why not be pro-active, and put in the resources early on so there is more of a chance to recognize difficulties before they turn into failure rates.

This takes the focus away from the student, and puts the responsibility firmly with educators, promoting equality of opportunity on access to courses.

A British perspective

The drop-out rate among students has always been of concern, and the attitude towards this situation can still be understood in terms of 'it must be the student that has the problem', typified by this quotation from Ryle (1969, p.45). 'Most writers agree that dropouts include a significantly high proportion of those with personality or emotional problems'.

Ryle then categorized the problems into four areas:

1. dropouts: students leaving permanently, without obtaining a degree;
2. interrupters: students taking time off their course for some non-academic reason, but eventually returning;
3. academic problem group: students identified as underachieving or in difficulty in the course of their studies;
4. failures: students who fail to graduate including those in categories 2 and 3 and students not previously identified as being in difficulty.

In category 4, we see that the problem is only noticed at the time of final failure, that is after examinations have taken place. This is precisely the context which this work is trying to challenge, by encouraging the identification of students with difficulties early on and developing a system of continuous feedback from students to tutors on their understanding of the course. The project also encourages students to take control of their learning, by providing the necessary framework. The Charter for Higher Education suggests that for students to reap the most benefit from teaching and learning, they must also take responsibilities. The wider participation rates which can be viewed by some to put a strain on the system and lower standards, can also be viewed as providing a rich mixture of traditional values that can provide a healthy tension. Universities need to examine their role in society with regard to the balance between relevance in courses and critical scholarship. We should be offering opportunities for the personal, social, emotional and cultural development of students, which are just as important as the intellectual (Caul, 1993).

DESCRIPTION AND PURPOSES OF SUPPLEMENTAL INSTRUCTION

The key features of SI, including addressing student concerns, are:

- SI is particularly targeted on 'preparation for learning' to equip students with the skills of academic enquiry, ownership of learning and the building of self-confidence.
- SI encourages the empowerment of learners to become autonomous in their learning in a managed environment but without direct staff input.
- SI recognizes that problems are often inherent in the courses themselves rather than in the students that take those courses. SI therefore targets high-risk courses and not high-risk students. It is therefore extremely effective at not only reducing failure rates, but improving performance across the board. The effects are demonstrably transferable to other courses that the students take. This transferability of skills gained in SI is of immense value.
- SI not only helps student's learning in the managed SI groups but is of great value to the student leaders who are carefully trained in the processes of group facilitation (*not* 'teaching').
- SI facilitates active student involvement and therefore provides an environment which research has shown to be one of the most effective for creating effective learning.
- SI is based on several years of extensive student evaluation work which has consistently highlighted student concerns about study skills and the need for feedback in the learning process.
- SI embeds study skills in the course material. This is significant

because all the available evidence suggests that the study skills training in isolation is not effective. SI empowers the students to be more independent and autonomous in their learning but does this in the most effective learning environment, that of well managed and interactive groups.

- SI is designed to embed learning strategy and study skills into course content *not* to encourage the learning of the 'subject' in isolation. This is achieved by processes of collaboration and co-operation among learners, by a system of supporting course tutors who invite the programme into their curriculum area, and then by training students to deliver part of this peer tutoring programme as facilitators of the group work.
- SI provides discreet support to practise a subject and is a safe place for students to discuss and process course material and openly admit their difficulties. The programme is also valuable in breaking down barriers between years. This results in learning co-operation rather than isolated competition.
- SI provides for successful transfer of skills which improves all round performance. Results have shown that the scheme offers opportunities for influencing institutional change.
- SI is of significant value across a very wide range of disciplines and institutions.

METHODOLOGY

Supporting the learner: preparation for learning

We have identified SI as a metacognitive approach. It encourages students to think about thinking, including knowledge about what we know and our ability to examine our processes of knowing, understanding, learning, remembering and reasoning.

If this can be achieved, it will lead to self-determination (or autonomy) in learning and problem-solving. This approach allows for the possible controlling of the how, when, where and why in learning, the knowledge particularly important in carrying out complex cognitive activities; the sort of activities that would determine and help target the difficult course for example. It offers a structured experience that enables critical and realistic reflection on what the learner is doing. It is a group-based project which is attached to specific high-risk or historically difficult courses (and therefore not remedial).

SI co-ordinator

The co-ordinators in SI are those people who most support the project in their institution. They might have a management function, or they might be an academic with particular responsibility for a year group (usually first year) or a subject area. The co-ordinator might also be from a central service such as an Educational Development Unit which is responsible for identifying targeted courses, gaining support from the faculty, department or school, and from individual staff. SI is offered where the tutor invites and supports the programme, and is looking at ways in which they can develop other ways of collecting feedback from their students. The tutor and the co-ordinator together select and screen the SI leaders for 'content competence' (i.e. that they have a sound understanding of the core principles of a subject) and recommend that they undertake further training. They are interested in student feedback and in trying out new ways of engaging students in the partnership of learning. The co-ordinator is also responsible for managing the SI programmes throughout the year, the monitoring and evaluation of the programme, and generally raising the profile of the project within their own institution. There is also provision for co-ordinators to meet with one another to compare experience, practice, and data through a national SI network. All of the co-ordinators take part in the two-day training session with the Student Leader. This is an opportunity for students and academic staff to share in the understanding and planning for the support of first-year students.

SI student training

The SI Leader, usually a second-year student who has been deemed course competent and approved by the course tutor, is trained in pro-active learning and study strategies. SI Leaders are also trained in interpersonal skills, team and group handling skills and a range of activities that enable them to improve their own management of group study sessions. SI Leaders prepare for the sessions based on the needs of their group, liaise with the tutor, attend weekly supervision with the SI supervisor and conduct one-hour sessions with designated SI groups. The SI Leader is a 'model' student and a facilitator who helps students to integrate course content and learning study strategies.

SI sessions

The SI group sessions takes place at a regular time, and in the same place, each week with the student leader taking full responsibility for the publicity of the sessions. Student leaders facilitate but do not teach, they encourage group members to solve their own difficulties from their own group resources. The leader then prompts the group to explore *how* they learn as much as *what* they learn. The material base is the students' own notes, course handouts, assessment materials and the recommended texts. Sessions are usually run only once a week due to the time restrictions and availability of space; they deal with the issues that students request. The sessions are not always about processing the last lecture attended, which would be the American approach, but rather deal with any problems the students might be having at the moment with a particular subject. This may be due to many factors, e.g.:

- most students in the UK are unable to attend the first-year lectures all over again as their timetable does not allow it;
- not all our teaching is through the medium of lectures and;
- some students will attend one or two first-year lectures, if time allows, to 'tune in' to the context again.

Liaison and partnership issues with academic staff

A focal point for SI in the UK is that the SI Leader is expected to feed back to the member of academic staff who is responsible for the course using SI. This partnership approach gives the student focused support regarding the content issues, and the academic is kept in touch with the real learning needs of their group. There will be indications of relevance of pace, understanding of the spoken word in the lecture, and the relevance of supporting materials. The student leader will be trained in the delicate art of negotiation during supervision sessions, as we realize it requires a special sort of skill, and courage, to be able to liaise with a member of academic staff.

Staff and educational development

The strongest development that the UK has made with SI is seeing it as a model for staff and educational development. Our concern in HE is that it is often the academic staff who may need to make changes in their practice, due to the changing nature of student intake and also that the curriculum offers are appropriate for current learner needs.

In the UK educational development usually has a central place in most HE institutions and, in the most progressive institutions, educational development is seen as curriculum development. The academic staff employed in areas that undertake development of education will be involved in the scrutiny of educational practice, so that hidden assumptions can be opened to question and challenged. The focus on the 'teaching-learning process' is significant in the sense that teaching and learning are two aspects of the same process, and that the process is the curriculum. In terms of this definition, primary value is attached to the knowledge and experience of both tutors and learners, and includes a focus on the beliefs and values which are inseparable from this knowledge and experience. Underpinning this definition is the understanding of education itself as a dynamic (as opposed to a static) process, involving continuous evaluation and redevelopment. The UK approach with SI is not only being aware of the multiplicity of ways in which students are disadvantaged on entry to university, but also while they are at university, through the content and teaching of the courses themselves.

SI in the UK is a vehicle for the stakeholders in the learning process – the students, the teachers and the developers representing the institutional need – to examine the learning process and outcomes.

CRITICAL ANALYSIS

Demonstrable benefits of SI

This project, which has been studied using action research methods, has recognized that the outcomes to date have been far richer than was originally envisaged. It was the enthusiasm of students and the collaboration and partnership of academic staff that have taken this work and developed it from an original American model to better meet the needs of learners in the British higher education system. The very nature of the changes we have made to the original US model are through staff development. Even though we have targeted the first-year undergraduate, to give support through peer tutoring, we recognize the partnership element of the programme plays a significant role.

Academic staff involved in SI become involved in the scrutiny of educational practice, and are encouraged to examine continually the curriculum through feedback from their SI Leaders. SI Leaders are trained and encouraged to work in collaboration with a nominated first-year tutor and, in their feedback from the SI groups, they become advocates for first-year learner concerns.

We gauged the extent to which the project has influenced staff attitudes or institutional approaches by the take up and running of pilot SI programmes. This was based on information gathered from an SI seminar and our publicity and published material. A number of universities have taken up SI during these past six years and all have reported various levels of success depending on their original intention. Much evidence was gathered during occasional SI co-ordinator workshops, where colleagues explored a range of issues, exchanging practice, challenging assumptions and sharing a general concern as to how to improve support to learners. We have also identified considerable interest from senior management in regard to the claims that this programme may reduce attrition rates.

Four major areas of benefit

1. The benefit to the *individual student* is primarily increased confidence and self-esteem which lead to the ability to master course concepts and to develop study and cognitive skills.
2. The benefit to the *student leader* is the development of a range of skills including team leadership and communication skills that they can then apply in other situations. They also gain a deeper understanding of their own subject area.
3. The benefit to the *academic staff* is that they receive regular feedback on how course content is being received by the learner. The process is one of staff development, arising directly out of managing the student learning process.
4. The benefits to *the institution* are that it is possible to target difficult courses and provide practical support for staff and students. The scheme improves student performance across the ability range and does more than simply reduce 'wastage' and 'failure' rates. The scheme provides a cost-effective way of supporting increasing student numbers and breaks down barriers between years to develop an effective learning community.

Student leader comments

The student leader is central to the SI initiative and continues to listen to what students are asking for in their learning. It has been the elements of student feedback that have helped to fine tune the developments in the UK. Here are some of the accounts from student leaders, which demonstrate that students, once given the responsibility, can organize, and make significant contributions to, their own learning.

One step taken by the staff when introducing SI to our course, which helped to ensure a lot of initial interest, was the polling of the class as to what subjects they felt that they would most like SI to cover. The response was very much as the second years predicted when asked but surprised some of the staff. This helped to reinforce the feeling that the second years were more in touch with the problems of the first years. Not surprisingly, the two topics that came out on top were both mathematically orientated and involved a lot of problem solving.

Simply attending most lectures and taking notes is often not enough for many students to succeed. They need to learn to interpret their notes and learn how to use them to solve the problems presented to them during their work. Coming from second-level education to the new world of the university can be a big shock. No one asks if they are doing their work like they did the year before and if they are presented with a problem they may not find everything they need to know to solve it in their notes. Even learning how to use text books or even choose them may be a problem. It is in areas like this that a senior student leader can be of invaluable help.

It is hoped that by teaching some of the basic skills needed to survive, the new students will soon learn to fend for themselves and prosper. It can be assumed that the students will soon learn these skills anyway, but the sooner that they acquire them the sooner they can begin to study successfully. Hearing tips from students who have already passed through the first year and achieved a relatively high standard is immediately encouraging.

This experience was nice in the first week as it helped me to see that I could help students save time struggling with simple problems that I had wasted time on in my own exam preparation. Also the students could see from this that I understood at least some of their problem and maybe they could see ways of using me to gain the most for themselves.

On doing well in their early phase tests, some students returned genuine gratitude for what they attributed to our input. These students were not held at bay in an SI session for the less confident. Warmly commending those on their input, I believe, was good for motivation all round.

The less confident were not quiet for long. A talking point for everyone and of great interest were the varied backgrounds of the students. The competitive atmosphere was somewhat relieved on realizing, as regards the course overall, that what was a piece of cake for one student was a painful nightmare for another ... and that if it appeared too complex at first this did not augur failure.

Recounting some of our experiences was of use. Usually being specific, we would give examples of assistance received from lecturers on subject matter, complex and apparently simple. What was important was not what was apparent but whether we really grasped the stuff or not. Consistency and a conscientious approach was the suggested formula. Letting a problem fester for too long was really just daft. Abruptness from lecturers was more probable if questions asked on dated material were not dealt with at the appropriate time.

To sustain successful SI sessions, the format had to be informal. To facilitate interaction and spontaneity, a certain degree of freedom had to abound. Motivation would prove difficult if a gulf existed between peer and student. In SI, nothing is lost in sharing knowledge with fellow students. The ability to communicate ideas orally (especially mathematically orientated material) was highlighted and related to areas of the course work such as project presentation, business orals and laboratory orals. Being conversant in the material, getting group feedback, and receiving approving prompts from the mediating peer were agreed to increase student drive. Simple things such as giving students uninterrupted flow in their explanations and avoiding rephrasing increased involvement.

The stating of our relationship to students was of major importance. We (the peers) were not lecturers, nor would we lecture. We were to be seen as fellow students with a year's experience and as allies. This avoided possible unpleasantness of lecturer-peer conflict. We were to avoid the appearance of setting ourselves up as better lecturers.

Limitations of the work

On reflection, the limitations of the work have been mainly political. Others' perceptions as to what it is and how it may be used, have created a climate where, at times, it has been quite difficult to proceed, therefore limiting the development of the work. This SI programme which is well established, has a built-in monitoring and evaluation mechanism, and its potential is easily measured. It is clear on purpose and is identified by well-defined principles. (Appendix 1). We therefore assume, because of its clarity of purpose and well-defined practice, that it has been an easy target for criticism. Unfortunately, it has attracted comments such as 'students could take the role of teachers' or even that this scheme 'exploits students'.

The reality is that this project has developed in an economic climate that sees an increase in student numbers and lessening resources. Students supporting one another can be seen as a cost-saving exercise. However, the project has built upon research which recognizes that students learning together in a collaborative and experiential way increases their learning potential. The Harvard Assessment Seminars (Light, 1990) conclude that students working in small groups of four to six learn slightly more as they seem to be more involved and enjoy it more.

After all, this approach is not new; children have always helped other children in the classroom (Topping, 1988). Monitors were used in Elizabethan grammar schools, and Andrew Bell and Joseph Lancaster in the late eighteenth century and early nineteenth century used children to tutor, with a view to educating both the tutors and the tutees (Goodlad, 1979). It builds on the foundations of good Primary School practice, and we would hope that approaches such as these should be incorporated into HE regardless of the economic climate. SI should be seen as a complement to the work of academic staff and a support to them in an era of increasing workloads.

Also, the project tries to dispel the notion that 'SI is a quick fix to all those answers'. What we have identified is that SI underpins and supports current good practice. It should not be the only learning support method on offer, but part of a range of offers that students are able to make choices from. When installing the SI methodology in a course, it will act as a kind of template. The strengths and successes are highlighted, but so too are all the weaknesses of the course.

The HEFCE report *SI Provokes a Teaching and Learning Debate* (1994) describes some of the ways in which academics have responded to a letter addressed to me suggesting that my work will encourage the use of more students as tutors, thus depleting the teaching workforce. The writer is one of many in our profession who believe that learning can only take place when the teacher is present! These eleven quotes from other responses to the letter are a reassuring vote of confidence from teachers who obviously understand the significance of peer tutoring.

For both groups of students (leaders and 'led'), SI provides a means to understanding better the process of learning. Students are therefore aided in the all-important skill of 'learning to learn' which is essential for continuing development throughout life.

Teaching in HE needs to be broadly conceived, and its tight association with learning, recognized. I believe it is possible to say that learning requires teaching and teaching requires learning and that teaching is done by many people.

We must define 'teaching' – most teaching conferred to students is lecturing – itself useful in its capacity to address large numbers of students effectively. However, it is apparent that with rising student numbers and limited resources, however cost-effective lecturing is, it has several fundamental drawbacks. Student attention is often very low; many spend much of the time dictating what is said verbatim and often fail to grasp the concepts being described. Any learning itself takes place not usually in the lecture theatre but in the students' ability to integrate uniformly prescribed and often sketchy notes into their knowledge base. Individual students have different learning needs which lecturing as a teaching method cannot address.

The 'power-gap' that exists between staff members and students is avoided. The more informal the environment, the happier the students will be to relate difficulties they have with the course.

Even if teaching is very good, students do not get 100 per cent; there is always room for improvement for students of all levels of ability.

The crucial difference is that teaching also involves the introduction of new facts, ideas, concepts, their explanation, and connections made – it is a moving on. SI facilitates consolidation, practice, clarification, revision and is looking back. It is true that this is the process that is important with the students themselves providing the content. Theoretically, an excellent SI leader could facilitate any subject, but that does not mean they could teach any subject.

SI leaders are not participating in the process leading to the award of a degree as they are not involved in any part of the assessment process. It could be argued that any person who works in the institution is part of the process from caretakers to cleaners as they are all involved with the process, if the points made are correct.

SI is a student-based effort at keeping higher education firmly in the grip of a broad educational ethos. It might therefore be better thought of as 'Supplemental Learning' rather than 'Supplemental Instruction'. This is the ethos of quality and, in particular, of the quality of students' conceptual understandings and problem-solving abilities.

Universities should be responsive to the widest possible range of customers and students. Widening access and participation in HE is all about redefining what 'capable' should and can mean in the HE context, and redefining how learning is best facilitated by universities and learners alike.

High drop-out rates can occur for a variety of reasons, e.g. the particular kind of supply into a particular subject (e.g. lower academic ability in many science/technology areas at the moment) or because of poor quality teaching, resources, ethos, etc. (these are a reality for which counter strategies are required). To assume that the remedy has to be better teaching is to make 'teaching' the a priori of learning, which it is not.

Why must we assume that all university lecturers have the professional skill of teaching?

FUTURE DIRECTIONS

The objectives for the future are to identify the developments of this work which have been developed and adapted to meet particular need. It is essential that adaptations are made locally, so that ownership of the process can be achieved. However there are key elements which should always remain at the core; for example, to target high-risk courses rather than high-risk students, so taking a pro-active approach to student support. The work is supported by training materials, which will continue to be updated.

   In conclusion, it is hoped that, wherever SI is used, it will generate a teaching and learning debate because, in our experience, it forces further thinking about whether the students are receiving the support they need.

APPENDIX

SI Principles

1. SI is a methodology for learner support.
2. SI is small-group learning.
3. SI is facilitated by other students.
4. SI is confidential.
5. SI is voluntary.
6. SI is non-remedial.
7. SI is participative.
8. SI encourages collaborative learning, not competitive.
9. SI is content based and process orientated.
10. SI develops integrating effective learning strategies.
11. SI works in the language of the discipline.
12. SI does not create dependency.
13. SI is pro-active, not reactive.
14. SI targets high-risk courses, not high-risk students.
15. SI encourages learner autonomy.
16. SI decreases drop-out rates.
17. SI gives opportunity to increase academic performance.
18. SI challenges the barriers between year groups.
19. SI benefits all students regardless of current academic competency.
20. SI gives privacy to practise the subject and make mistakes and build up confidence.
21. SI enables a clear view of course expectations.

REFERENCES

Arendale, D. and Martin, D. (1994) Review of research concerning the effectiveness of supplemental instruction from the University of Missouri-Kansas City and other institutions. *Resources in Education* (ERIC Clearinghouse on Higher Education) October, ED37 0502.

Barnett, R. (1992) *Improving Higher Education: Total Quality Care.* Buckingham: Society for Research into Higher Education and Open University Press.

Caul, B. (1993) *Value Added.* Belfast: December Publications.

Department for Education (1993) *The Charter for Higher Education.* London: DfE.

Goodlad, S. (1979) *Learning by Teaching.* London: Community Service Volunteers.

Haselgrove, S. (ed.) (1994) *The Student Experience*. Buckingham: Society for Research into Higher Education and Open University Press.

HEFCE (Higher Education Funding Council for England) (1994) SI provokes a teaching and learning debate. Bristol: HEFCE (Northavon House).

Light, R.J. (1990) *The Harvard Assessment Seminar: Explorations with Students and Faculty about Teaching, Learning and Student Life*. Cambridge, MA: Harvard University Press.

Martin, D.C., Blanc, R.A., and De Buhr, L. (1983) Breaking the attrition cycle: the effects of supplemental instruction on undergraduate performance and attrition. *Journal of Higher Education* **54** (1), 80–9.

Rust, C. and Wallace, J. (eds) (1994) SI: helping students to learn from each other, Paper 86, Staff and Educational Development Association, Birmingham.

Rye, P.D., Wallace, J. and Bidgood, P. (1993) Instruction in learning skills, an integrated approach. *Medical Education* **27**, 470–3.

Rye, P.D. and Wallace, J. (1994) Helping students to learn: supplemental instruction. *Student British Medical Journal* **2**, 79.

Ryle, A. (1969) *Student Casualties*. London: Penguin.

Topping, K. (1988) *The Peer Tutoring Handbook*. Buckingham: Croom Helm.

Wallace, J. (1992) Students helping students to learn. *New Academic*, **1** (2), 8–9.

Wallace, J. (ed.) (1994) *HEFCE Project Report*. Bristol: HEFCE (Northavon House).

A disabled student in higher education: moving beyond segregation

Peter McDonald

Medical treatment, human knowledge, technology and collective resources are already such that our physical or mental impairments need not prevent us from being able to live perfectly good lives. It is society's unwillingness to employ these means to altering itself rather than us, which causes our disabilities. (Stephen Duckworth, quoted by W. Finn, 1995, p.14)

A society which isolates and excludes so many people and has them at its margins is living in denial. Our communities are all diminished by exclusion and segregation because it denies us the full range of human diversity and human experience. (Evelyn Pellow, 1995)

INTRODUCTION

I was born in Jamaica in 1965. I was born with cerebral palsy, which in my case meant that I could not walk, had poor hand-eye co-ordination and I frequently had involuntary muscle spasms, particularly in my legs. My mother taught me to read and write, as I did not attend any school until after arriving in England in late 1971. I had to undergo a battery of tests to establish my educational fitness, to decide what sort of special school I was capable of attending; (it would be over ten years before anyone suggested that I might be able to attend a mainstream school or college). At the age of seven, having only my mother's teaching in Jamaica, I had the measured reading age of a fifteen-year old. In 1990, after a number of near disasters and a lot of luck, I gained a degree in sociology.

It is not a lack of ability which limits disabled people. It is a fundamental lack of opportunity to demonstrate their capabilities and talents. My experience of education leads me to believe that people with disabilities generally do not benefit from segregated education, and society as a whole has been warped and distorted by this artificial division of the education system.

WHAT IS DISABILITY?

Although there are a number of variations on the theme of disability theory, two 'models' of disability may be outlined: the medical model of disability, and the social model of disability (Morris, 1991; Oliver, 1983; 1990).

The medical model sees the problems of disabled people as a direct consequence of their medical condition, and the supposed limitations of this condition. Although social resources and medical intervention may aid the 'disabled person', or attempt to compensate for his or her 'loss', the problem is essentially seen as something for each disabled person to deal with. Rehabilitation and adjustment are primarily the responsibility of each individual. (This is sometimes viewed as a passage through a number of 'fixed' psychological stages.) Using this paradigm, society can reduce its responsibilities towards people with disabilities. Such provision can be seen as the care and maintenance of a disadvantaged minority, while the main structures, practices, attitudes and beliefs of society in relation to people with disabilities are likely to remain unchanged.

The social model emphasizes the need for fundamental change in the negative attitudes generally held by society towards people with disabilities, as we are portrayed in literature, the mass media, historical and religious texts, plus the widespread segregation of disabled people from the 'non-disabled' (at all levels of society), which both promotes and reinforces stereotypes, prejudice and discrimination against people with disabilities.

> It is not simply a case of prejudice (or the lack of prejudice), but it is a case of whether people working within a given environment are sufficiently aware of the effects that their typical behaviour, or everyday activities may have on other people. The simple act of defining some people as 'disabled' and other people as 'normal' will automatically deprive some people of the opportunity to form relationships in whatever way they might choose. In practice, the assumptions that often underlie the concept of disability will mean that some people are allowed only a limited range of physical or social environments, with only limited choices and rights.
> (McDonald, 1992a:1)

Having experienced ten years of segregated education, there is no doubt in my mind that the medical model is dominant within special schools. The model often seems to be combined with an assumption that a broad education, placing appropriate emphasis on academic competence and the development of skills, is not required by disabled students, because the state can be expected to look after them for life.

The most damaging aspect of the medical model is that it tends to assume that human potential and ability cannot supersede the functional (medically defined) limitations of our bodies or our minds. This model provides much of the justification for the existence of special education itself.

PHYSICAL AND SOCIAL ISOLATION IN SPECIAL SCHOOLS

From the time I was seven until I was sixteen, I went to the same school, travelling several miles in an adapted school bus. As a child I did not realize how isolated my school was, not only from the community where I lived, but also from the communities that were nearest to the school itself. Years later I learned that it was common practice to build special schools in isolated locations, away from large communities.

I remember few opportunities to develop contacts or common activities with other schools. Almost all of these contacts were with other special schools. Excluding family members, all of my friends were disabled people, or at least people whom the medical and educational establishments had defined as being disabled enough to attend my school. These definitions seemed to include a wide range of people, from those with severe forms of cerebral palsy, spina bifida or muscular dystrophy, through to people whose only reason for being there was that they experienced rare bouts of epilepsy. Even in the 1970s, it was clear that some pupils were in special schools simply because of the ignorance and prejudice of those in mainstream education.

Segregated education perpetuates the general invisibility of people with disabilities throughout society. The concept of disability itself becomes separated and isolated from the experience of wider society, so that non-disabled people learn little or nothing about the experience of disability from disabled people themselves. It becomes natural and logical if you rarely encounter people with obvious disabilities in mainstream schools or places of work, than you rarely consider us as friends, partners or colleagues in everyday life.

Segregation of any kind perpetuates the development of myths and stereotypes, which easily develops into a fear or prejudice against those who are perceived as being fundamentally 'different'.

HIERARCHIES OF DISABILITY

I believe that, throughout human history, it has been common practice to associate beauty, athleticism and physical strength with moral and social superiority. Much of the mass media, particularly the advertising industry relies on common insecurity about appearance, physical abilities or sexual prowess to promote and sell their products to people who can usually be regarded as medically healthy. A sense of inadequacy is often deliberately generated by comparing average men and women with film stars, athletes and supermodels. The conceptual link between beauty, health and moral superiority is commonly expressed in children's stories; we accept that the wicked witch, the villain or the pirate, must have some deformity or a missing limb, which we frequently associate with deviancy, or as a sign of evil intentions or madness (Goffman, 1968; Morris, 1991). Fiction and cinema aimed at adults frequently uses disability or deformity in much the same way as it appears in fairy stories. The typical villains in the James Bond films, or numerous horror movies, offer just a few examples of the very negative way in which disability is portrayed to society as a whole.

> The way disability related issues are presented in the media is not only offensive to disabled people but is also a major barrier to integration. Just as racist or sexist attitudes, whether explicit or implicit, are acquired through the 'normal' learning process, so there is evidence that 'disablism' is learned in this way too. (Barnes, 1994, pp.196–7)

These negative attitudes can be absorbed by anyone who is exposed to them, whether they consider themselves as having a disability or not.

I have many fond memories of friends, fellow pupils and teachers. My schoolmates and I were probably at least as likely as anyone else to dare each other, to boast of our skills and abilities, play practical jokes on each other (and the teachers, of course) or to support and defend each other in time of need. The school also had its share of bullying, name-calling and occasional bouts of gang membership, from the nursery to the senior classes, whereby one's particular disability, race or any other distinguishing feature was likely to be used as a target.

Despite the fact that we were all in the school because of our supposed disabilities, I believe we all felt the need, particularly at times of stress and uncertainty, to develop 'hierarchies of disability' whereby we could prove (according to our own logic) that although we might be more disabled than some, we could also demonstrate to ourselves that we were less disabled than others. Therefore, in some ways at least, we could argue that we were better than other people.

I do not believe that most of our teachers were aware of these hierarchies. Because they were unaware of them, they could make no effort to challenge them, or to debate these issues with us, their pupils. In addition, I remember few (if any) discussions about negative images of disability in books and the mass media, or societal prejudice against disabled people, which affected us all to some degree.

PERSONAL DEVELOPMENT AND NEGATIVE SELF-IMAGE

Because of my family background, I was always encouraged to think educationally, to compensate for being Black and having a disability as well, to compensate for the unknown prejudices and negative experiences that I vaguely knew were out there, but had been sheltered from in segregated schools. To cope with the disadvantages that were perceived in being in a sheltered, unrealistic environment of a 'special' school, I was always encouraged by my family to study twice as hard as anybody else. However, I do not feel that the education I had at special schools gave me opportunities to find out what I wanted to do as a person, what I wanted to achieve. I always felt at a disadvantage to any pupil who had been through the mainstream system, where I believed they were never discouraged from thinking of themselves as fully fledged future adult citizens, qualified members of the economy and society.

> As a child with cerebral palsy, I was pre-occupied with surviving in a special school. Jamaica often seemed a very long way from my classroom and from my experience of disability. Day by day, my awareness of race came second to my awareness of disability, because it seemed the most practical way to deal with life. I was struggling to find my own identity, or at least a positive image of myself, instead of the many negative images I was being asked to choose from.
>
> Whenever the subject of race came up at home, someone would

remind me that as a black person who was also disabled, my chances of achieving anything in life were probably less than zero. It was my 'destiny' to suffer twice discrimination and to miss twice as many opportunities as the person who was 'only' black or 'only' disabled. (McDonald, 1991)

I was lucky enough to leave school with three O-levels and two CSEs, which was about the maximum number of subjects available at my school at that time. Most of the pupils in my year left school with no qualifications. In my opinion, if all the pupils in that year were encouraged in previous years to think that study and exam passes were a possibility for them, most of us would have left school with more to show for the time we spent there.

FEARS AND MISCONCEPTIONS

For many years, I believed that integration in education was virtually impossible for disabled students to achieve. I firmly believed that bad attitudes, the negative beliefs and concepts held by both non-disabled people and people with disabilities alike, would be impossible to break down, with little hope for the future, and few possibilities for meaningful relationships between the two groups.

> ... if society rejects and excludes people with demonstrable differences ... how are we to explain individuals and social groups who come to accept, like and love others with the most profound disabilities? (Taylor and Bogdan, 1989, p.22)

> There exists a role of 'disabled person' distinct from the fact of having a disability and any genuine limitations that disability may impose, which we are expected to adopt and conditioned to conform to. (Sutherland, 1981, p.71)

Because of the negative beliefs I held, it took me several years to develop the confidence to approach those who were, in effect, on the other side of the fence. The transition from segregated to mainstream education, in my case, required more change in my own negative attitudes, than any medical changes or technological developments.

TAKING A RISK

After a particularly unsuccessful year at a residental special college, my careers officer decided to take a chance – a big chance – by getting me a place at the local (mainstream) further education college. This was a major turning point in my life. The college had virtually no facilities in terms of access or special equipment for people with disabilities. There was certainly no formal disability awareness among the staff members or students. However, seemingly by chance, there seemed to be a fundamental willingness among both students and staff to allow me to negotiate my own position, to give me the room to explore my own potential. The general attitude of both staff and students might be summarized as follows: 'We don't know how to help you, we haven't got the facilities, but if you want to succeed, we want you to succeed, and we will support you in any way we can in order to help you to succeed. We will learn about you at the same time as you learn about us, and together we'll get through.'

A MATTER OF LUCK

I believe that I benefited greatly from a number of chance events. I was probably the first disabled student ever to attend my FE college. I feel that this gave me a certain novelty value (in the best sense of the word) which generated a degree of enthusiasm for my presence at the college. In addition, I was very happy to be there, and I think my attitude communicated itself to staff and fellow students. Second, I strongly suspect that none of the staff members had any connection with the special education system, therefore they did not carry many of the medically based attitudes that seem to be fundamental to those who were trained as part of the special needs system. This meant that I was the primary source of information on all disability issues relating to my situation, on a daily basis. Being the main source of disability awareness in a large college, however, is a heavy responsibility for any individual, no matter what their background. I had to be much more assertive (when identifying my needs to other people) than I had ever been before. I also learned to be more assertive (and less diplomatic) when refusing assistance that I did not want or need. I learned that humour is a valuable tool when negotiating awkward situations while causing the minimum amount of offence.

LEARNING HOW TO BE A STUDENT

Coming from a segregated education system, I quickly realized how poor were my basic study skills, such as note-taking in lectures, essay planning and writing, and time-management. I had not been taught these skills, and they were rarely demanded of me by special education. My time at the local FE college (doing O- and A-levels) gave me an essential opportunity to develop these skills, under less pressure than I experienced at university.

By the time I reached university, I had developed a good memory for facts and figures, which partially compensated for the fact that I had always found writing with pen and paper a slow and tiring process, because of cerebral palsy. If I concentrated too much on note-taking during lectures, I often found that I would miss points and issues which were being spoken while I tried to write down other things. Soon I virtually gave up on note-taking, in favour of listening, asking questions frequently, and memorizing essential details. I also spent a great deal of time between lectures in university libraries, not only making notes for essays or projects, but also making notes that the other students might have made during lectures, from papers and textbooks that my tutors had used, or recommended to me.

Most of my A-level essays were handwritten, a process which normally took me about twice as long as most students I knew (not including planning or reading time), because of the physical difficulty I had with writing. Fortunately at university I had frequent access to word-processors, which dramatically accelerated my work-rate. Word-processing also improved the quality of my work, because it allowed me more time to plan, re-draft and develop each project more fully.

I also had to consider practical issues, such as allowing myself extra time to reach classes, as the lifts frequently broke down. I did not use my wheelchair often, but relied chiefly on a pair of metal walking sticks. I have always found the process of climbing stairs slow and tiring, and certainly not the best preparation for a lecture or seminar. Occasionally, a lecturer was able to move the class to a more accessible location, when the circumstances allowed it, but such re-locations did not happen often.

Generally speaking, both further and higher education were much more demanding (both physically and mentally) than anything I had experienced in special education. Because of my experience at A-level, in a mainstream college, I developed the confidence and ambition necessary to take on a degree. I would not have had the confidence to attempt going to university, if I had not gone to a mainstream college first.

RELATING TO STUDENTS AND LECTURERS

> When able-bodied and physically handicapped individuals meet,
> the nature of the interaction will be determined by the stereotyped
> notions the able-bodied individual holds about physical disability
> and the handicapped person's way of coping with such attitudes.
> (Lynn Leahy, 1982, p.9)

Within weeks of enrolling at my local FE college, I began to realize
that most non-disabled people (taken on a person-by-person basis)
were not as alien and unapproachable as I had often feared that
they would be. Although a small number of students seemed to
want to avoid me, or spend as little time with me as possible, most
were in fact were very curious about me, my disability and my way
of life. I quickly learned that the vast majority of students that I
encountered had little or no direct contact with any disabled
person before meeting me. Questions on every conceivable topic,
from what I was studying, to whether I had sexual intercourse (and
if so, how did I manage it), became everyday topics of discussion
between myself and the students who were getting to know me.

Some students were not interested in making friends. However,
they were often still keen to find out all they could about me, as the
only disabled person that they could approach to ask about disability, or what the experience of disability was like. Some students
(and lecturers, for that matter) asked all the questions they ever
needed to raise within the first five minutes of meeting me, and
having satisfied their need for information, rarely (if ever) raised
the subject of my disability again. Other students (and lecturers)
felt the need to return to the subject many times during my years as
a student, whenever they encountered issues or potential problems
which they had not previously considered in relation to disability.

After giving a lot of thought to my situation, I made the decision
to answer these questions as openly and honestly as I could, so
long as I felt there was a genuine need for information, for the
following reasons:

1. It gave me an opportunity to state my personal point of view on
   a vast range of subjects which influenced my way of life. This
   was an opportunity I rarely had during my time in special
   schools.
2. I hoped that it would encourage other people to see my disability as one part of my total personality and experience, rather
   than something which must inevitably dominate all other
   aspects of my life. I reasoned that at some stage in our relationships, my fellow students would realize that I had much more to

offer as a human being than just my disability, and that most of my hopes, dreams and ambitions were similar to their own.

3. Some students were initially nervous about approaching me or becoming friendly with me because of their fear of doing or saying anything which I might find offensive in relation to my disability. By taking the initiative, by being frank and open about myself, I believe that I managed to avoid several possible misunderstandings, while hopefully demonstrating that I was an approachable, friendly human being.

4. During my years at college and university, I was told that a small number of other disabled students were later studying at these establishments, as a direct result of my presence. Most of the time, however, I was alone as a disabled student, and most of the time these establishments relied on me to educate both students and staff about disability issues, and also to raise the general level of 'disability awareness'.

WHAT IS DISABILITY AWARENESS?

An absolute definition of disability awareness is difficult to achieve, because it is partly based on subjective interpretations. However, there are at least four common elements, drawn from many discussions and from research involving myself and other people with disabilities (McDonald, 1992b). When taken together they may increase our understanding of what disability awareness involves.

1. The desire and ability to communicate effectively with people who have a disability, and to work towards an understanding of their concerns.

2. The desire and ability to respond to the concerns of people with disabilities in positive and appropriate ways.

3. The desire and ability to avoid patronizing or discriminatory practices or behaviour, in relation to people with disabilities, at both the individual and group levels.

4. The desire and ability to consult people with disabilities on all policy matters which may affect them, ideally before such policies are implemented.

THE FEAR OF GETTING IT WRONG

Being seen as the main source of information on disability issues in a large establishment, and a source of inspiration to other students, often became very heavy responsibilities to bear on my own, no matter what the reasons for taking on these tasks. I had a tremendous amount of fun, in spite of frequently being exhausted by the physical problems of moving around buildings that were not designed with disabled people in mind. I very much enjoyed the constant challenge of meeting (and sometimes exceeding) the same academic requirements as those faced by my fellow students. I was pleased and honoured to have earned both respect and friendship from students and staff members.

However, I was always aware in my own mind that my successes or failures might have some influence over the support that was offered to other disabled students who came after me. I felt that I was put under tremendous pressure to set a good example; I pressurized myself, in the hope of making this better for other students with disabilities who might follow me into higher education.

CONCLUSIONS

I have learned from experience that integrated education involving students with and without disabilities sharing the same curriculum and classrooms, is possible and raises the levels of mutual awareness and understanding, if there is sufficient will, imagination and dedication on all sides to allow it to succeed. Even with current buildings and facilities, I believe that there are many practical steps which can be taken which would allow many more people with disabilities to be successfully integrated into mainstream education in the near future.

The first, and most cost-effective of all measures should be to consult directly and frequently with disabled people about what they want and need to maximize their potential and to enhance their experience of education. It is also vitally important to employ and train people with disabilities at all levels of the education system and in all tasks within the system, so that their expertise can play an essential part in turning the long-term dreams of integrated education into reality.

Many of the most positive aspects of my experience in further and higher education were almost entirely dependent on the goodwill and imagination of all concerned, and my personal capacity to relate to and communicate with others. There was rarely any planned effort to integrate me, or to provide additional facilities or finance, beyond that which was available to other students.

While an individual's capacity for self-integration can vary tremendously according to personality and the needs arising from disability, it is unwise and unjust to leave so much of the process to chance. Longterm planning and funding initiatives need to be developed, not only for improved access and facilities in all schools and colleges, but also to provide disability awareness training to all teaching staff. Disability awareness also needs to be included as a fundamental feature of the National Curriculum for all pupils.

Genuine opportunities for education can and should be available to everyone in society, not just those we would like to define as the 'most able', or 'the brightest and the best'. Such élitist attitudes tell us next to nothing about future ambitions, potential, or contributions to society. Such élitism and segregation can only tell us about the limitations and handicaps that some parts of society would like to impose upon others.

REFERENCES

Barnes, C. (1994) *Disabled people in Britain and discrimination.* London: Hurst.

Finn, W. (1995) Ready willing and able. *Intercity Great Western Magazine,* February, 14–18.

Goffman, E. (1968) *Stigma: Notes on the Management of Spoiled Identity.* Harmondsworth: Penguin.

Leahy, L. (1982) *Barriers to Intimacy for People with Physical Disabilities.* Norwich: Social Work Today/UEA.

McDonald, P. (1991) Double discrimination must be faced now. *Disability Now,* March, 8.

McDonald, P. (1992a) The experience of the Black child who is disabled. Unpublished conference paper, presented at Child Protection and Children with Disabilities, a one-day conference held at the NSPCC National Training Centre, Leicester.

McDonald, P. (1992b) The employment of people with disabilities within the Spastics Society. Unpublished report. The Spastics Society has changed its name to Scope.

Morris, J. (1991) *Pride against prejudice.* London: The Women's Press.

Oliver, M. (1983) *Social Work with Disabled People.* London: Macmillan.

Oliver, M. (1990) *The Politics of Disablement.* London: Macmillan.

Pellow, E. (1995) (Editorial): No one should be excluded, *Special Needs,* March, 3.

Sutherland, A. (1981) *Disabled We Stand.* London: Souvenir Press.

Taylor, S.J. and Bogdan, R. (1989) On accepting relationships between people with mental retardation and non-disabled people: towards an understanding of acceptance. *Disability, Handicap and Society,* **4** (1). [Paging not available.]

Equal opportunities and access: developments in policy and provision for disabled students 1990–1995

Alan Hurst

INTRODUCTION

In the last fifteen years there has been a major concern with widening participation rates in higher education by under-represented groups. Most of the focus has been on women and on some minority ethnic groups. Disabled people have been rather neglected. This can be seen in a number of reports on access (e.g. Ball, 1990; Fulton and Elwood, 1989) and, although as I hope to demonstrate below, some progress has been made, more recent publications continue to indicate the same lack of regard (e.g. Farish *et al.*, 1995). Making progress has not been helped by having little information about disabled students in terms of both quantitative (O'Hanlon and Manning, 1995) and qualitative data (Hurst, 1993). The situation is improving and statistics are available now from both the Higher Education Statistics Agency (HESA) and from the Universities and Colleges Admissions Service (UCAS). For example, Table 9.1 shows some details based on information provided by applicants using the appropriate section on the UCAS form in 1994.

While such figures are of interest, their value is limited. On the face of it, disabled applicants accept places in the same proportion as those who apply. However, there is a danger that by using the categories based on disability, the focus is shifted away from a social model of disability towards an individual/medical one. (For a discussion of models of disability, see Chapter 3 in Oliver, 1996.) What the figures do not reveal is the extent to which students encounter barriers at particular institutions and with particular

Table 9.1   *UCAS Applications and Acceptances (1994)*

Disability	Applications		Acceptances	
	Number	%	Number	%
Dyslexia	2,991	0.7	2,003	0.7
Blind/partially sighted	510	0.1	308	0.1
Deaf/hearing impaired	962	0.2	644	0.2
Wheelchair user/mobility	406	0.1	265	0.1
Personal care support	69	0.1	32	0.1
Mental health difficulties	216	0.1	107	0.1
Unseen disabilities	11,521	2.8	7,724	2.9
Multiple disabilities	415	0.1	273	0.1
Other disabilities	1,331	0.3	854	0.3
Total with disability	18,421	4.5	12,210	4.5
No disability/no reply	386,696	95.5	258,688	95.5
Overall totals	405,117		270,898	

Source: CVCP, 1995.

courses/subjects. One explanation for the figures could be that disabled students are very thorough in their preliminary research and apply only to those institutions which have the facilities they need and where there is a strong chance that a place will be offered. Summarizing the statistics from HESA, it is clear that most disabled students are full-time rather than part-time, most are undergraduates rather than post-graduates, and most are in institutions formerly funded by the Polytechnics and Colleges Funding Council (PCFC) rather than the Universities funding council (UFC). There is a further important element missing from the above, namely quality. While an indication of success of any efforts to widen participation might be an increase in numbers, this does ignore the quality of the experience. In more recent times, there has been an increased concern with 'quality' and yet the needs of disabled students seem to have been excluded so far.

Having set the scene, the rest of this chapter will review the progress made in improving opportunities in higher education for disabled people. I begin by looking at how developments have occurred which affect students and then at those affecting institutions. The closing section considers the potential impact of anti-discrimination legislation on higher education.

DEVELOPMENTS AND CHANGES AFFECTING STUDENTS

The major development affecting most disabled students is the relatively better financial situation following changes made to student grants. In 1990, when top-up loans were introduced, the government also introduced modifications to the Disabled

Students Awards (DSA). Since 1990, students have been able to claim a general allowance, an equipment allowance, and an allowance to pay for non-medical personal assistance. The amounts available for each have increased annually in line with the rate of inflation.

While many disabled students have benefited enormously from this extra funding, there are some serious problems associated with it. First, for some, the money available is not enough to meet their needs. Second, DSA are not available to all disabled students; some are excluded as a result of the operation of the means test on the income of their parents, and post-graduates are also excluded. However, the biggest excluded group are part-time students. Figures from HESA indicate that of the 26,270 disabled under-graduates on courses in 1994, 6360 were part-time. For many of them, part-time study might be the only option available as a result of their disability. The attraction of part-time study for disabled people is shown by the success of the Open University. To include any part-time students in the system of student awards requires legislative changes and recent governments have been unwilling to allow time for this. Doubtless they also fear the increase in demand which could follow.

Another source of concern stems from the operation of the system itself. Funds for DSA come from central government but are administered by the local education authorities (LEAs) which seem increasingly conscious of their accountability for public money. At present, pending the creation of unitary authorities, there are between 100 and 120 LEAs and they operate in different ways. Some practices are helpful to students but many others create additional difficulties (e.g. by asking for estimates of costs before agreeing payment, by insisting that students first obtain the services or equipment and then reclaim costs, by slow processing of applications so that students do not have access to the services/equipment at the start of their courses). Many of these problems were identified some time ago (Patton, 1990) but they continue to pose difficulties.

A particular feature to emerge is the large number of students claiming DSA on the grounds of having a specific learning diffi-culty (dyslexia). This came as a major surprise both to the institutions and to the LEA. Somewhat unusually, the situation here is one where some people seem keen to secure a 'disability' label because of its access to additional funds and services. In contrast, other people try to avoid such a label because of its nega-tive connotations. (An article entitled 'Brainwaves' published in the *Guardian* (17 October 1995) opens with pictures of six well-known public figures and the text 'Dyslexia does not equal disability – who would dare to call these six people disabled?') To be fair to LEAs, there have been some instances where both individual students and some institutions have been trying to abuse the system, although not to the extent reported in a front page article in *The Sunday Times* (10 September 1995). In this article, entitled 'Universities face enquiry on low-IQ entrants' an LEA awards officer is reported to have said that: 'Many students who excused their academic failures by claiming to have dyslexic tendencies did not suffer from the condition. The vast majority of those claiming grants were not dyslexic she claimed.'

In March 1995, the Department for Education (DfE) announced its intention to review DSA. A letter was sent to a small number of organizations (but not to institutions) seeking responses to a number of questions concerned with LEA publicity, definitions, systems, etc. Some of these give cause for concern and suggest that the Department is worried about the growing costs of DSA. For example, a question about students' use of special equipment following completion of their courses could indicate that the Department was considering savings by collecting equipment already purchased and re-distributing it.

The responses to the Department were interesting. Skill (National Bureau for Students with Disabilities) highlighted four key issues in its overall approach: the support needs which DSA should and should not cover; the responsibilities of the higher education institutions themselves; inconsistencies among LEAs especially on assessments, and required evidence; and problems created by delayed payments. An organization representing the LEAs (Association of County Councils) felt that more direction was needed from central government and also that more liaison between interested groups would be useful, but the response is adamant that there was no cause for concern about inconsistencies. However, particular attention is drawn to issues relating to dyslexia. The response from the Committee of Vice Chancellors and Principals (CVCP) appeared to indicate that most issues could be resolved by others rather than by anything that it might do. The CVCP response focused heavily on what LEAs might do while the matters which institutions could address seem to be totally ignored.

In late July 1995, the newly created Department for Education and Employment (DFEE) included information about DSA in its interim report on its review of further and higher education; (see below) (DFEE, 1995). One interesting section indicates the costs of DSA and shows that the overall cost rose from £2.10 million in

1991–92 to £6.02 million in 1993–94. This rise is clearly of concern and the publication of the DFEE review is awaited with some apprehension by those working with disabled students; see Chapter 10 by Cooper and Corlett for a discussion on DSA.

DEVELOPMENTS AND CHANGES AFFECTING INSTITUTIONS

For many years some institutions have been trying to develop high-quality provision for disabled students. The speediest progress was made in those institutions which were formerly polytechnics. Much was accomplished although there was no financial incentive to do so. Funds to support work with disabled students had to be taken from current operating budgets. Many institutions did little or nothing, preferring to use their resources for more prestigious activities. Also, if some were doing something for this group of students, others felt they had no need to act. The provision of funds to institutions to encourage the less-committed institutions and to ensure that those already incurring costs do not feel that they are penalizing themselves by doing so is the issue for discussion.

Following the creation of a more unified system and a single funding body under the Further and Higher Education Act 1992, the then Secretary of State for Education declared that the councils had to pay some attention to the needs of disabled students. (Here it is necessary to point out that there are separate councils for England, Northern Ireland, Scotland and Wales and each has implemented the Secretary of State's wish differently.)

The Higher Education Funding Council (England) (HEFC) established a small Advisory Group on Access and Widening Participation. Skill was invited to represent the interests of disabled students on this group. In early 1993, it was announced that £3 million was to be made available to support the development of policies and provision for disabled students. Institutions were invited to bid for funds to support their own individual projects, the bids being judged against pre-determined, published criteria. Institutions could submit two bids if they wished. Over 100 bids were received, of which 38 were given support. In making its choices, the Advisory Group was conscious of the need to encourage those embarking on provision with those already with experience and anxious to make further progress. Skill was invited to play a key role in monitoring the projects and in disseminating information deriving from them. Since there were significant projects relating to deaf students and to dyslexia, special meetings were called for representatives from these projects. In addition, a termly booklet was produced and circulated. Also, to further dissemination, all projects had to submit an annual report to HEFC and, on the basis of the information provided, an overall review was published (HEFC, 1995).

Despite criticism of both the funding methodology and the timing of the special initiative, the procedure was repeated for the 1994–95 academic year. Again £3 million was available, although it was made clear that institutions could not make bids simply to continue their previous projects since these should have become embedded within the existing structures and practices. From the 91 bids, 49 were selected for support and Skill was asked to play a key role in the monitoring and disseminating of information.

The complete two-year strategy is the subject of an overall evaluation with the publication of a final report by the HEFC in early 1996. Even now, it is possible to identify a number of outcomes. On the positive side:

1. Although many of these involved with the projects are members of networks of practitioners, there has been an increase in the number of events at which people can meet to exchange ideas, information and experiences;
2. While all the formal events have been evaluated by their organizers, what is often missed in this process is the value of informal contacts made during tea breaks, lunch intervals, etc.;
3. There has been an upsurge in the production of materials concerned with disability in HE – pamphlets, guidebooks, reports, videos, posters, etc.;
4. The projects have contributed to raising awareness about disability;
5. Many institutions have made progress in developing their policies and provision and thus extending the choices available to disabled people;
6. Some of those where progress has been made have tried to ensure that what has been accomplished continues beyond the life of the project.

Turning to more negative aspects and linking to the last point above:

1. As the end of the projects approaches, it is becoming evident that some institutions do not intend to continue with the work despite exhortations from HEFC to have regard for this when making the original bids;

2. Dissemination has been only partially successful especially in terms of its impact on the non-funded institutions and of sharing information and avoiding duplication of activities – not all projects have sent contributions to the termly newsletter compiled and circulated by Skill, and not all institutions sent representatives to the October 1994 national dissemination conference;
3. Issues relating to the need for staff training have emerged so that, in early 1995, Skill organized events directed towards a quick induction for staff new to working with disabled students;
4. In producing regular reports, projects, perhaps understandably, have seemed less willing to record their difficulties and failings although this is crucial if others are to benefit from their experiences and avoid the same problems.

It is appropriate at this point to offer some description of projects supported by HEFC.

HEFC PROJECTS: TWO CASE STUDIES

The two case studies which will be described in detail have been chosen because their foundations are rather different. The project initiated at the Sheffield Hallam University was arguably the only one built upon a clear conceptualization of the issues involved, whereas the project based at the University of Central Lancashire is more typical in many ways in its being rooted in pragmatism.

Sheffield Hallam University

The main aim of the project at the Sheffield Hallam University was to undertake a systematic audit of what the university had available to support disabled students and how the development of a new framework could enhance provision. The project encouraged the close involvement of disabled people, mainly students but also a small group of disabled staff. It differed from most other projects in making clear its basis in key principles. First, it made a clear statement about the social model of disability and the social oppression resulting from this; see the earlier reference to Oliver, 1996. While many other projects and institutions subscribe and uphold this view, the team at Sheffield Hallam gave it great emphasis. Second, the team was keen to recognize disability culture. Within this, the importance of the experience of disability, self-definition, self-determination, and self-advocacy were acknowledged.

As its starting point, the project team took the principles of independent living identified by disabled people and then applied them to the context of higher education. The definition of 'independence' is concerned with the extent to which disabled people/students are in control of their own lives and are able to organize them in ways they want. Also important is the idea of 'choice' – having a range of possibilities and being able to decide for themselves.

The first of the seven principles is about information and access to it. Thus, for blind students, materials should be easily available in the format which they desire – Braille, pre-recorded cassettes, personal readers, of a combination of these. Access to information is also a matter which concerns deaf students. For example, information should be made available through the use of British Sign Language. No matter what the nature of the disability, the concern here is with the total 'information environment'. It would be wrong to assume that what is at stake here is access only to teaching and learning. In fact, it involves every aspect of university life from having admissions information produced in several formats to ensuring that news of events in student social life is transmitted effectively.

The second principle relates to peer support. The experiences of other disabled students can be of considerable benefit if they can be shared with others. The project team made great efforts to secure the involvement of disabled students in their work. In particular, an introductory programme was devised to try to encourage participation from disabled students right from their first arriving at the university. One intention of this was that the early involvement would lead to greater participation in the existing procedures – for example the Disabled Students Forum.

The third principle of independent living is about housing. As with almost all universities, there is a shortage of accessible, affordable accommodation. Many institutions have developed adapted facilities especially in their halls of residence. However, the cost of living in the halls are high and many students cannot afford the rents. For some students, this may be the only possibility and yet, by choice, they would like to live with friends in flats, rented houses, etc. The project team recognized the right to live where the individual chooses. To this end, they suggest that universities could try to become more influential in their approaches to local authorities and to housing associations to ensure that a suitable choice of accommodation is available in the local area.

Moving to the fourth principle, the project team affirmed the right of disabled students to technical aids and the equipment they need. This links with the earlier discussion about the DSA and about who it encompasses and who it excludes. One important point noted at Sheffield Hallam is the need for independent, informed advice about equipment appropriate to the individual's needs. While recognizing this, in terms of the earlier definition of 'independence', a disabled student is free to ignore advice. Buying specific items of equipment might not be compulsory although for example if IT equipment has been chosen and recommended for purchase because of its compatibility with institutional systems, ignoring advice could lead to difficulties.

Fifth, in addition to equipment some disabled students need personal assistants. Trying to meet the needs of disabled students has involved many different universities in a variety of schemes. Some choose to use Community Service Volunteers; others have appointed their own staff specifically for this work. For the Sheffield Hallam team, the only solution which accords with the principles of independent living is one where the disabled student has direct control over those who are providing the assistance. The personal assistants become the employees of the individual and are there to do those things for which there is no other means available.

The sixth principle relates to the environment. To achieve independence, disabled students have the right of access to all facilities. In many universities, this has become possible since a gradual programme of conversions and adaptations have met the needs of disabled people. However, problems still remain. Thus, while access to buildings is possible, it is not always by the most direct, most convenient or most generally used route. Also, in HE, geography and architecture present other barriers. Many buildings occupied by the older universities have protected status and so any plans to improve access are received cautiously. Some newer universities are campus-based rather than city-centre sites and thus the layout of the campus and its location *vis-à-vis* other public facilities is important. The former polytechnics are often based on several sites or use buildings some distance from each other; this too creates difficulties. In fact, Sheffield Hallam University is an example of the latter and the team was very much aware of the need to consider geography and environment in their own work.

The final principle of independent living used by the Sheffield Hallam project team concerns transport. They reaffirm that disabled people have the right to accessible, affordable public transport. This becomes of some significance when considering both inter-site travel within institutions and travelling from a campus base to a nearby town. There is considerable evidence about the lack of access to public transport in this country. In 1993, London Transport publicized its decision to 'open' the Underground system to more disabled people, especially to wheelchair users. In truth, of the 270 stations, only about 40 are totally accessible and most of these are in the suburbs where the trains run on the surface rather than in central London. On the main railway system, British Rail is moving only slowly to improve access to the network for disabled users. On buses, more attention is being paid to the needs of visually impaired passengers, although in only a small number of places are bus services totally accessible to wheelchair users.

In case it appears that the discussion has wandered from its main purpose, consider the situation in Champagne-Urbana, Illinois, USA. There the University has gained a reputation for its policies and provision for disabled students. The large number of disabled students has contributed to major improvements to the public transport system. All buses are accessible to wheelchair users and so they can travel where and when they want. In England, totally accessible public transport is in its infancy although, to bring the discussion right back to the focus, it is interesting to note that disabled staff working at the Sheffield Hallam University have been involved in the design and development of the rapid transit system recently introduced into the city.

University of Central Lancashire

While those working at the University of Central Lancashire would subscribe to the principles outlined above, the recognition is more implicit than explicit. In fact, the HEFC Project at Central Lancashire was based on a long-standing commitment towards welcoming disabled students; for details of the development of policy and provision see Hurst, 1990.

The 1993–94 application aimed to fill gaps in the existing provision. Thus, while the university could give support to blind students, services for deaf students were at a low level. The university applied for funds to appoint a full-time communicator. This was linked also to the development of Deaf Studies as a subject within the Combined Honours Degree Programme. A second group of students whose needs were not being met were those with specific learning difficulties. This situation was made worse by the large increase (unanticipated) in the number of students claiming to have a specific learning difficulty. Funds were required to employ both a part-time psychologist to undertake the assessments necessary to allow access to the DSA, and also to employ a specialist support tutor. Third, based on the university's Specialised Learning Resources Unit (a team of staff based in the Library and working mainly to produce classroom materials in formats appropriate to the needs of disabled students), funding was requested to employ additional technical and clerical staff. Finally, some funding was requested to be used as bursaries to support the needs of part-time students. The total sum asked for was £70,000 and this was approved in full.

In implementing the proposals several issues emerged:

1. The number of students claiming to have a specific learning difficulty was such that the services of the educational psychologist and the specialist support tutor could not meet the demand.
2. The growth in the number of deaf students, each following a different course, meant that employing one communicator was impractical. Permission was given to use the services of a local organization which could meet the demand when deaf students were timetabled in different classes at the same time.
3. The demand for bursaries demonstrated the extent of needs among part-time disabled students.

At the end of the year, the university employed an experienced, external consultant to evaluate the project and to make recommendations for future action.

A further bid to HEFC was made for 1994–95 which tried to build on what had been achieved and also tried to look ahead to ensure that project gains could be sustained and fully embedded into the institution. Funding was sought to pay the costs of staff cover to allow an experienced member of the Disabled Students Advisers team to create registers and to recruit suitably qualified and experienced people from the local community who would be available to offer support to students with a range of needs – audio typists, readers, specialist tutors for students with specific learning difficulties and so on. Such a system was seen to offer a flexible resource to cope with an unpredictable demand and avoids the university itself employing staff who might become under-utilized. Funds were required also to allow the senior technician based in the Specialized Learning Resources Unit to develop stronger links with the National Federation of Access Centres with a view to the university becoming a full member or being given accredited status so that assessment of students' equipment needs for DSA purposes could be undertaken 'in-house'.

The university wanted to appoint a specialist careers officer; having been successful in recruiting disabled students, it has become essential to give more consideration to their employment needs at graduation. Looking to the future when money from HEFC would no longer be available, the university proposed to appoint a specialist marketing officer/fundraiser to try to secure the additional money needed to maintain the improved levels of service. Finally, in an attempt to ensure that work with disabled students is given the recognition it deserves and also in an effort to disseminate ideas, the university proposed to work with other institutions to develop a course and a qualification for staff working with disabled students in HE. Had the HEFC agreed to support everything, the total cost would have been £95,000. However only £70,000 was allowed, the university itself agreeing to meet the shortfall.

Progress was made with all dimensions of the bid, although with more problems than in 1993–94. Recruiting a careers officer took until Spring 1995 and so this dimension of the work only began in April. However, even in the short time since then, some important matters have been addressed, in particular participation in networks with other specialist careers advisers and with employers' groups. The appointment of a fundraiser took even longer and so the financial security which was hoped for has not yet been achieved. In relation to both posts, the university has adopted what might be regarded as a 'whole institution' approach. The two post-holders have been placed in the 'mainstream' services rather than with the Disabled Students Office for line-management purposes. The efficiency and effectiveness of this have yet to be determined.

Progress with the other dimensions of the bid has been clearer. The university has been visited and audited in relation to its application for recognition as an Access Centre while, in October 1995, a Post-Graduate Diploma in Professional Development (Higher Education Disability Services) was validated successfully. This is the first course of its kind and has been devised and developed with staff from over a dozen other institutions. It will be delivered using a balance of work-based learning and residential sessions. A number of awards will be available ranging from a University Certificate for those new to the work or with only limited experience while the more enthusiastic might continue to master's degree level. The content has been organized around six modules, each of which tries to balance practical skills and substantive knowledge relating to disability and HE.

It is time now to return to the broader context and to look at how more recent events have implications for policies and provision for disabled students in higher education.

THE CHANGING NATIONAL CONTEXT

In England, in the mid-1990s, there has been a major concern with trying to eliminate discrimination on grounds of disability. At one time, in 1995, there were two separate proposals for legislation under discussion in the House of Commons. One was more radical and emphasized civil rights but this was 'talked out' during a debate on July 13th since there was insufficient time to discuss the 168 amendments proposed by the government. The other proposals, sponsored and supported by the government are less radical. The main areas of concern are access to goods and services, employment and public transport. This means that discrimination in education, for example at the point of entry to university, is not illegal. Although education is excluded, much pressure has been exerted to force the government into making some changes.

Related to this, the government has asked the DFEE to undertake a review of further and higher education. The latter is to consider the role and responsibilities of the HEFC, the quality of teaching and learning, DSA (see the earlier references to this), the Students' Charters, and the work undertaken by Skill.

However, even before this review has been published, the government has proposed amendments to the 1992 Further and Higher Education Act. The first will place a statutory duty on the Funding Council to demonstrate that it has considered the needs of disabled students in its allocation of funding. This really strengthens the Secretary of State's request from 1992. The second amendment will require all HE institutions to publish statements about their policy and provision for disabled students. Further reference to these amendments will follow shortly. Before that, it is interesting to spend a little time considering how the government's proposals were received and how they have proceeded through parliament.

The debates in the House of Lords revealed some interesting perceptions. Matters which have been of concern included definitions of 'reasonableness' in relation to adaptations to buildings and the consequent expenditure:

> Who decides what is 'reasonable'? We shall have to work out the answer to that. The noble Lord asked for an undertaking that nothing in the Bill would pressurise a university to change the

content of a course. I should think that such a decision would be entirely for the university. However, it might be legitimate to ask a university to ask itself whether there was another way of arriving at the same course with the same content and of the same standard. (Baroness Darcy De Knayth col. 1999 Hansard 15 June 1995)

Allied to this concern with costs the 'centres of excellence' approach reappeared:

It is obviously important that higher education, as education generally, should make adequate provision for all those who, by reason of disability, may not be able to find a suitable place and to vary provisions in order to assist them ... It is important that there should be some place; it need not necessarily be that every institution must provide a suitable place. (Lord Beloff col. 874 Hansard 22 May 1995)

Clearly, if this idea was implemented it would restrict choice and limit opportunities, a point noted in the response of another Lord:

On access and the whole issue of higher and further education, I ask the Minister to consider, within presumably the coherent programme the Government seek, as opposed to what the Minister described as the piecemeal approach ... perhaps developing different facilities at different universities to allow student choice. That is fine for students who are able to leave home and students of standard entry age. However, an increasing percentage of students are mature students or students who have physical problems which do not allow them to leave home. Therefore it is important that all higher education institutions are adapted as quickly as possible. (Baroness Farrington of Ribbleton col. 1995 Hansard 15 June 1995)

Another major concern is to protect the autonomy and academic freedom of the universities:

... the genuine and important needs of disabled students are being used, on occasion, for the Government to go back on a decision reached by Parliament that the one thing the funding council may not do is to place conditions on the grants affecting academic matters ... The difficulty is that once a provision of this kind is overridden on a worthy cause, what will stop the Government from coming forward and providing means of over-riding it for some less worthy cause? (Lord Beloff col. 876 Hansard 22 May 1995)

Hopefully, these very brief extracts from the parliamentary debates convey something of the variables introduced into the debate.

Even before the appearance of the anti-discrimination legislation, and the changes associated with it, HEFC has taken action. In Autumn 1995, a small subgroup was created the sole concern of which is students with disabilities and learning difficulties. The role of the subgroup is to offer advice about the format and content of the disability statements required from every institution and to explore strategies for funding institutions on a more permanent basis for the work they undertake with disabled students.

With regard to the disability statements, the references so far have been quite vague, although in the debate in the House of Lords the government's spokesman was more expansive with regard to similar statements required from FE institutions. He suggested that the statements should include information on physical access, facilities, etc. In fact, this information for higher education is available already in several sources. It would be a pity if the new statements are to be a repetition of this. Much more valuable would be some kind of development approach indicating how institutions intend to make progress with what they already have. With regard to funding, the incentive of financial recompense should encourage institutions to develop their policies.

The existence of this subgroup is to be welcomed and bears witness to the progress made. While the situation might not yet parallel that in Australia where the government has published national guidelines on aspects of policy and provision for disabled students (NBEET, 1994) it is a move in the right direction. The more general anti-discrimination legislation together with the specific changes in education offer real grounds for optimism and suggest that, in the near future, disabled students will be able to participate fully in higher education and with fewer difficulties.

REFERENCES

Ball, C. (1990) *More Means Different: Widening Access to Higher Education.* London: RSA.

CVCP (Committee for Vice Chancellors and Principals) (1995) *Briefing: Universities and Disabled Students.* London: CVCP.

Department for Education and Employment (1995) *Further and Higher Education Review Programme: Disability Discrimination Bill – Interim Report.* London: DFEE.

Farish, M. (1995) *Equal Opportunities in Colleges and Universities: Towards Better Practices.* Buckingham: Society for Research in Higher Education.

Fulton, O. and Elwood, S. (1989) *Admissions to Higher Education: Policy and Practice.* Sheffield: Training Agency.

HEFC (1995) *Access to Higher Education: Students with Special Needs.* Bristol: HEFC.

Hurst, A. (1990) Obstacles to overcome: higher education and disabled students. In J. Corbett (ed.) *Uneasy Transitions: Disaffection in Post-Compulsory Education and Training.* Basingstoke: Falmer.

Hurst, A. (1993) *Steps Towards Graduation: Access to Higher Education for People with Disabilities*. Aldershot: Avebury Press.

NBEET National Board for Education Employment and Training (1994) *Guidelines for Disability Services in Higher Education*, commissioned Report No. 29. Canberra: Australian Government Publishing Service.

O'Hanlon, C. and Manning, J. (1995) *Students with Disabilities and Special Needs: Applications for Higher Education in 1993–94*. Birmingham: University of Birmingham.

Oliver, M. (1996) *Understanding Disability: From Theory to Practice*. Basingstoke: Macmillan.

Patton, B. (1990) A survey of the disabled students allowances. *Educare*, **36**, March, 3–7.

SHEFC (1994) *Access to Success for Students with Disabilities in Higher Education in Scotland*. Edinburgh: SHEFC.

Sunday Times (1995) Universities face enquiry on low-IQ entrants. 10 September.

10

An overview of current provision

Deborah Cooper and Sophie Corlett

INTRODUCTION

Higher education for people with disabilities has changed rapidly over the last few years. More is available to, and more is expected by, disabled students in the mid-1990 than was dreamed of by most disabled students in the mid-1980s. This chapter looks at some of those changes in the context of wider development in post-compulsory education. It also provides an outline of how one organization, Skill, has been involved in bringing about changes for the better and increasing the opportunities that exist.

THE CHANGING CONTEXT OF POST-COMPULSORY EDUCATION

In the 1970s, when the Warnock report was being prepared (DES, 1978) a study was carried out to look at opportunities for so-called 'handicapped' pupils following compulsory education. The results were given in the report and were one of several pieces of evidence given at the inaugural meeting of Skill: National Bureau for Students with Disabilities (then called the National Bureau for Handicapped Students) in 1974. The problem described was one reason why the organization was so needed. As Professor Peter Mittler from Manchester University said on that occasion: 'Some three quarters of pupils leaving special schools were thought by their head teachers on good evidence, to be able to benefit from opportunities of further education, and yet only a quarter of these pupils were able to enter further education' (NBHS, 1974:12).

The then Minister for Disabled People, Alf Morris MP, at the same event, referred to a student who had recently had to delay starting his course because the only landlady offering accessible accommodation was ill. These were two of many examples of the lack of opportunity for young disabled people in further and higher education.

During the 1970s and 1980s, doors in FE began to open. This was partly because colleges became more aware of their role as establishments that should reflect and respond to their local communities. It was also helped, perhaps, by other changes, including the loss of certain groups of students including those on apprenticeships.

Legislation followed this initial growth and perhaps encouraged the trend. The 1988 Education Reform Acts for the first time made direct reference to students with learning difficulties. This legislation was superseded by the 1992 Further and Higher Education Act and 1992 Further and Higher Education (Scotland) Act which built on the 1988 Act and resulted in considerable interest by the new FE funding bodies in students with learning difficulties and/or disabilities. As a result the current funding regimes in England, Wales and Scotland all recognize the additional costs of this provision. The inspection systems also recognize this as an important area of provision.

This interest within further education has had at least two important influences on opportunities in higher education. First, the increased opportunities for students to study for qualifications have provided a greater pool of students to transfer to higher education. Second, the different funding methodologies, inspection frameworks and structures to guarantee learning support have offered a useful starting point for higher education.

It was this interest in developing opportunities in post compulsory education and training that led to Skill being set up.

Skill's role

Skill was set up in 1974 to try to increase opportunities for people with any kind of disability in education, training and employment. The initiative started as a result of research into opportunities in higher education, which showed few opportunities and little support was available. Interest quickly spread to further education when those involved realized how much the two sectors depend on, and interact with, each other.

Skill works towards its objective through activity in three different areas: advising individuals, promoting good practice and monitoring and influencing policy. Skill currently advises over 5000 individuals a year, about half of whom are students, the rest being professionals working with students, family members or other supporters. The numbers of enquiries have risen steadily and have doubled in the three years from 1992 to 1995. The increase in enquirers is both encouraging and discouraging. In part it is good to know that more students are aware of Skill's service and are able to contact an agency which can answer their queries. But unlike, say a bookshop, Skill does not seek an increase in clients. Skill does not see itself as a supplementary specialist service that exists because other services do not know how to deal with disabled people. Nor does it want to replicate the work that should be carried out by statutory agencies. On the contrary, Skill's long-term aim is to make sure all the usual statutory services, such as careers services, education authorities and institutions themselves have the right information to meet the needs of disabled people. Skill needs to respond efficiently and effectively to the existing needs of individuals but, in the meantime, it wants to make that information available to others who are closer to the individual students.

Information work goes hand in hand with Skill's work on encouraging good practice. It is not enough for students to have the knowledge about what or where they wish to study only to find that once they start applying, institutions are unable or unwilling to support their needs. Currently educational establishments are still able to choose not to accept students on the grounds of disability and there is evidence of discriminatory practice once students are accepted. For example, students have contacted Skill because they have been turned away from courses to study teaching or medicine because of their dyslexia without any discussion of the severity of their condition or the implications of any strategies which they might be using to overcome it. A deaf student already on a course, who needs to use a small piece of equipment called a radio aid in lectures, was prevented from doing so because her lecturer refused to clip on the tiny microphone. Extreme examples like this are rare, but they illustrate a lesser, more widespread, inflexibility in attitude and practice in many HE institutions.

Professionals do not always realize that their policies or practice are restrictive to disabled students. Skill's role is not to condemn those who have not begun to change, but to encourage better practice among all professionals and to provide practical help in the process. Skill produces and disseminates written material, including the *Skill Journal*, outlining good practice and new developments across the UK. It also provides opportunities for practitioners to learn from and inspire each other through conferences and workshops and through the local HE networks which meet termly across England and Wales. As in its information work, Skill does not see itself as standing centre stage, but rather acting as a catalyst for practitioners themselves to develop their own expertise and to be involved in change.

Both bad and good practice are affected, and to some extent determined, by the national policies on educational provision and, most powerfully, by the legislation that controls the distribution of funds. Skill's third main area of work is monitoring and influencing such policy to realize an administrative and legislative infrastructure that would make equity automatic.

The most crucial way in which this can be effected is through legislation itself. The work which took place during the passage of the 1992 Further and Higher Education Act and the 1992 Further and Higher Education (Scotland) Act is an example of how this can be done. Skill first made contact with senior civil servants and politicians as soon as the rumours about a possible White Paper began to circulate, and was again in touch once the White Paper was published. It was at this early stage that Skill began to work out exactly what it wished to achieve through the legislation, who it might work with to secure any necessary changes and what financial and staff resources would be required. Skill has a history of working in close partnership with other disability groups, and again on this occasion Skill was in early contact with a number of other agencies. Working with others has a number of benefits, chief of which are the greater resources which are available when several organizations pool their staff and expertise, and the greater impact which a combined voice can have on the civil servants and politicians with whom Skill works. As a result of this combined activity, the Bills when they were first published already had direct references to students with disabilities and learning difficulties in FE. Lobbying of MPs and peers and continued work with civil servants meant that by the time the legislation received royal assent promises had been made in relation to HE too. As a result, the new bodies which were established by the Acts to fund further and higher education were given encouragement by ministers to consider ways of increasing participation by disabled students. This has led to each of the funding bodies in England, Wales and Scotland taking initiatives in relation to these students.

More recent legislation (the 1995 Disability Discrimination Act) has provided Skill with equal measures of frustration and opportunity. The legislation outlaws discrimination in a number of areas such as employment and the provision of goods and services, but from the start excluded education from its overall scope. Once again Skill, working in consultation and collaboration with other organizations, lobbied civil servants and politicians to secure amendments which would provide a better framework for improved provision in post-16 education.

Skill's effectiveness as an organization can to some extent be measured by the changes that have occurred in policy and practice within the sector.

THE LEGAL FRAMEWORK FOR HIGHER EDUCATION

Higher Education institutions have no specific legal responsibilities towards individual disabled students. And unlike FE funding councils, the HE funding councils are not able to prescribe certain standards or policies within the institutions which they fund.

HE institutions have a large degree of independence from the funding councils and this extends to the way that they respond to disabled applicants and students. Over the years, this has proved to be both a strength and a weakness: some institutions have used their freedom to develop excellent and groundbreaking facilities; others have seen this latitude as a licence to do nothing at all. As a result discrimination still persists, and there is no real sanction against it. But in the last two years there has been increased encouragement from the funding councils to improve facilities through a number of special initiatives. These have speeded up the process of change, and are outlined in more detail below.

The Disability Discrimination Act, however, has given the HE funding councils new duties. These are outlined below:

A duty to 'have regard to the requirements of disabled persons'

The HE funding councils in England, Scotland and Wales are required to consider the needs of disabled people in 'exercising their functions'. In other words, at each level of their work, in their funding decisions and in their other 'functions' such as quality assessment, the funding councils are required to consider the implications for disabled students. The HE funding councils were asked at their establishment to seek ways of improving the participation of under-represented groups including students with disabilities, and much of the activity over the last few years has stemmed from that request. This duty is now enshrined in law and, as such, mirrors the duty that has existed in FE since the 1992 FE and HE Acts, which has led to a number of useful changes at a strategic level in that sector.

A duty to require HE institutions to publish 'disability statements'

This new duty is being imposed on the funding councils in HE and FE. The disability statements are intended to incorporate information about institutions' policies and provision for disabled people and may also include an outline of any plans institutions have for upgrading provision in the future.

These duties are as yet untried, and it is yet to be seen what effect they will have. The hope is that taken together the new duties will give the HE funding councils both the information and the power to take a more strategic role in encouraging good practice.

THE DISABLED STUDENTS' ALLOWANCES (DSAs)

No overview of provision in higher education would be complete without mention of the DSAs. These are part of the mandatory award available only to disabled students who have additional disability related study costs. The allowances aim to meet the costs of students' individual needs, not the costs of the university infrastructure or support. There has been an allowance available for many years but it was originally a fairly small sum which was not widely publicized among those who might have had need of it. As a result of campaigning by Skill and others during the passing of the Education (Student Loans) Act in 1990 the allowance was uprated and expanded into three linked allowances. At present (1995) the levels of the DSAs stand at:

- £4850 maximum per annum for non-medical personal helpers – this might cover for example an amanuensis, sign language interpreter or an assistant to help with practical work;
- £3650 maximum *over the course* for equipment – this might cover a radio aid, or a specially adapted computer; and
- £1215 maximum per annum general allowance to cover any smaller costs or, if necessary, to supplement the other allowances.

The advent of the uprated and expanded DSAs have had a dramatic effect. Students who previously could never have considered going to university because of the expense of their support needs suddenly could afford to do so. Whole groups of students with particularly expensive support needs, such as deaf students, had previously been restricted to studying at a few institutions who had made particular efforts to accommodate them; now these students could select the university, and thus the course, of their choice.

DSAs are not without problems, however. In England and Wales students apply to their local education authority (LEA) and in Northern Ireland from their education and library board for the allowance. There have been great discrepancies between the ways that different awarding authorities have dealt with applications and the expenditures which they have considered to be legitimate. In Scotland, where all applications are made through the same body problems in this respect have been correspondingly less. A further problem has arisen because of late payment of allowances by authorities, leaving students without the funds they need in the crucial first weeks of a course. The Department for Education and Employment has begun to address these problems through guidance and a more recent review, but there is a long way to go before the system runs as smoothly as it should.

More fundamental are the problems which arise because of the limited scope of the allowances. DSAs are supplementary allowances attached to the mandatory award and are therefore available only to those who are eligible to claim a mandatory award. This means that students taking a second or post-graduate qualification, and more commonly, those studying part-time are not eligible to claim. It also means that some students find their allowances are affected by the means test. As a result, and despite the apparent generosity of the allowances, there are still students who find that they have no realistic means of paying for the support they need (see also the discussion on DSA in Chapter 9 by Alan Hurst).

THE ROLE OF THE FUNDING COUNCILS

Changes in legislation, the work of Skill and the pioneering work of some institutions have all played their part in raising awareness of the needs and skills of disabled students. As a result, the pace of change has gained momentum. The funding councils have been pivotal in benefiting from and contributing to this process.

All three funding councils, the Higher Education Funding Council for England (HEFCE), the Higher Education Funding Council for Wales (HEFCW) and the Scottish Higher Education Funding Council (SHEFC) have responded in different ways to the ministerial instruction to consider widening participation for disabled students.

England

The large number of institutions in England, and the enormous gaps between the level of provision for students with disabilities in the best and the worst of these institutions, posed a real challenge for the HEFCE. One of their first moves was to set up an advisory committee on Widening Participation to look at ways of increasing participation by disabled students and students from ethnic minorities. For the first group, disabled students, the result was two separate one-year 'special initiatives'. In both years, the sum of £3 million was set aside from the funding council's budget and made available to institutions through a bidding process for projects relating to disabled students. Preference was given to institutions which could show an existing commitment to disabled students. Thirty-nine projects at 38 institutions were chosen to receive funding during the year 1993–94. The projects covered a range of areas: some focused on specific groups of students such as deaf students or students with mobility difficulties; others looked at specific areas of institutional life such as the admissions process or staff development. Several of the projects concentrated on students with dyslexia. To minimize overlap and duplication, institutions were urged to communicate with each other and disseminate their findings. Skill was asked by the HEFCE to assist in the process of dissemination.

For the second initiative in 1994–95, HEFCE requested that bids put a greater emphasis on how project gains would be embedded within institutions. Forty-nine new projects were selected, some of them from the same institutions as the previous year. Again Skill was asked to help with dissemination, and institutions were enjoined to make their findings widely available.

There have been drawbacks to the initiatives not least the short-term nature of the funding; some institutions have found that they had not made arrangements to embed project gains adequately into the institution before the project came to an end and funding ceased. But the overall result of the two years' activity has been a huge leap forward for many institutions who were able to progress work which might in other circumstances have taken several years to develop. Although there have been institutions that have neither had funding nor significantly benefited from others' projects, the special initiative has meant a general move forward for the sector. Provision for disabled students now holds a higher profile and is more widely accepted as an integral part of institutions' overall provision.

Wales

The smaller number of institutions in Wales (there are just 14) initially prompted a different approach by the HEFCW. In 1993–94, £2 million was allocated to 'academic infrastructure' which was distributed to all the institutions on a pro rata basis. Institutions were given guidance on the type of expenditure which might be appropriate under the heading academic infrastructure, one of which was provision for disabled students. However, only one third of institutions did, in the event, choose to spend the funds in this way. In 1994–95, therefore, the HEFCW decided to go through a bidding process along similar lines to the English initiative for projects specifically aimed at students with disabilities and seven institutions eventually received funding. In 1995–96 HEFCW returned to the academic infrastructure model, but also made available a further £1 million which was earmarked for capital academic infrastructure work to benefit disabled students.

Scotland

It was acknowledged that few Scottish institutions had the level of provision of some of the institutions south of the border and so in 1993–94 the SHEFC decided to conduct an audit of provision and policies for disabled students in Scotland. One of the audit's findings was the importance of the role of disability co-ordinators in facilitating the entry and support of disabled students. In response to this, SHEFC decided in 1994–95 to part-fund the posts of new disability co-ordinators in each of its institutions and to fund one central co-ordinator for the whole of Scotland. At the same time, it made available £2 million to fund equipment resources to be set up by the institutions working together on a regional basis. The effect of these two initiatives was striking. Several institutions which previously had no systematic approach to disabled students began to develop policies. Institutions began to work together to share ideas and approaches. In order to consolidate this success, SHEFC has continued to fund the co-ordinators into 1995–96.

Northern Ireland

In 1994–95, the two universities in Northern Ireland (which has no funding council of its own) also received funding to improve provision for disabled students. Here too, the extra funding has given a signficant boost to the level of provision available to disabled students.

THE ROLE OF NETWORKING

One factor which has been instrumental in setting and increasing the speed of change over the last few years has been the collaboration and networking between staff concerned with provision for students with disabilities in different institutions. The first Skill network was set up in the North West of England by a Skill member who saw the benefit of those with a similar role but possibly very different skills and experiences meeting to share their expertise. Since that first network was set up in 1987, other networks have been established so that there is one within easy reach of disability co-ordinators from any institution in England and Wales. Almost without exception co-ordinators have been willing to offer free advice and support to their colleagues in other institutions, and the networks have operated as a source of inspiration and staff development to old and new co-ordinators alike.

The shortage of disability co-ordinators in Scotland until recently had meant that earlier attempts to establish Scottish networks had been unsuccessful. However, networks have now been established by the SHEFC-funded national co-ordinator and these have already proved to be as useful as those in England and Wales.

There are also now more specialist networks in operation looking at areas such as provision for deaf students, or co-ordinating provision in a specific locality. These too are having an impact on the level of provision in the sector overall.

The effect of these networks and the goodwill that underlies them cannot be overestimated. The pace of change under the special initiatives of 1993–94 and 1994–95 has made if difficult for networks to keep up, but their very existence has meant that the sector has benefited many times over from each project. It is an irony that the spirit of competitiveness which is now encouraged in HE institutions to increase their effectiveness, if it had reached this group of professionals, would have undermined this rich source of support.

WHERE ARE WE NOW?

Progress over recent years has been considerable. Provision has moved forward: there have been advances in the understanding of how some conditions, such as dyslexia, affect academic work; there have been exciting breakthroughs in the technology available to disabled students; there have been developments in systems and procedures for making provision within institutions; more is known about what constitutes 'good practice' in such provision.

While moving forward, progress has also been outward: more institutions consider disabled people as being part of their constituency; more institutions have policies and provision for disabled students; within institutions themselves, more staff have an interest in, and understanding of, and are taking responsibility for, the support of disabled students.

Yet not all recent developments have been for the better. The spotlight on disability has raised the profile and acceptance of these issues, but it has also brought to light questions which at best are unresolved and, at worst, prompted the sector to view disabled students with greater suspicion.

One of the more contentious issues concerns dyslexic students. Dyslexia, or more precisely, specific learning difficulties, has always been with us, but since the enhancement of the DSA in 1990 the numbers of students coming forward to declare their dyslexia has been increasing year on year. Better support for people with dyslexia during compulsory schooling, the availability of computer software which helps students to work around their dyslexia, and the lessening of the stigma surrounding dyslexia may all account for this increase. But some people have more cynically suggested that many of those declaring dyslexia do not, in fact, have significant specific learning difficulties but are simply hoping to claim DSAs to buy computer equipment, or are wanting to gain concessions from the university authorities to cover up their low intellectual abilities.

Whatever the reasons, the huge increases in numbers have led to suspicion from DSA awarding authorities which may, in the long-term, be detrimental to the interests of these students. Some academics too have doubts about how dyslexia impacts on academic standards and institutions have, in some cases, been almost overwhelmed with the extra workload and responsibility which rising numbers of dyslexic students have brought with them. Again, there is a danger that institutions may begin to look less sympathetically at dyslexic students in the future. The sector is beginning to address this problem to some extent; in early 1995, a group of educational psychologists and others with an interest in dyslexic students set up a working party under the chairmanship of Dr Chris Singleton, of the University of Hull. The group hopes to examine the way dyslexia is diagnosed and draw up ways of distinguishing between mild dyslexia which would not merit extra funding or support, and specific learning difficulties that may have a more significant effect on an individual's study.

The dramatic increase in students with other disabilities have also led to practical difficulties. There have been logistical problems in meeting the needs of so many students, particularly at busy times during enrolment or examinations. In some cases, there have been no realistic ways of meeting students' needs at all: the increased numbers of profoundly deaf students needing sign language interpretation has outstripped the supply of qualified interpreters in the country, and many institutions have found they can only offer less appropriate forms of support such as notetaking. This type of difficulty is an inevitable consequence of the pace of change, but requires a solution nevertheless.

The additional funding available for provision for disabled students both through the special initiatives and through the increase in the DSA has also led to some institutions reducing their own financial commitment towards disabled students. Since the uprating of the DSA in 1990, a few institutions have begun to use the allowances to fund aspects of their service. Some students are being charged not only for the interpreter or computer or notetaker which they use or buy, but also for the person who arranges the hire or purchase. Some students are being asked to pay towards the help received from institution staff in claiming the allowance in the first place. The additional presence of specially earmarked funds during 1993–94 and 1994–95 to spend on provision for this group of students has led to some institutions withdrawing their own funding for disability co-ordinators, special support facilities, and supplementary tuition. Many institutions make a major financial commitment to disabled students, but their efforts are, to some extent, undermined by those whose approach is less wholehearted. The lack of clarity between the different sources of funding needs to be addressed if institutions are to be on an equal footing, and if students across the sector are truly to gain maximum benefit.

Changes in the wider HE environment too are not all for the best. The development of modular courses has been beneficial for many disabled students who have been able to tailor make their course to suit their own needs and to study at the pace which suits them. This might be particularly valuable for students with disabilities which are fatiguing, such as ME. But as choices become wider the individual support which students receive from course tutors or personal tutors is often reduced. This can make the HE experience confusing and disorienting for any student, but for a student who may need to co-ordinate a sign language interpreter a term in advance, or for someone with dyslexia who finds it difficult to plan their time, the lack of consistency in support can be devastating.

And there are ongoing problems which still need to be addressed. Many part-timers and others who may not claim DSA are failing to benefit from the advances across the sector because they cannot afford to enter HE at all. And there is an entire group of institutions which have simply not participated in the changes and developments across the rest of the sector. There is no real way of forcing institutions to improve their provision for disabled students. Indeed, without legislation that outlaws discrimination on grounds of disability in HE, there is no way of requiring a certain standard of provision from anyone. Discrimination against individuals, and against groups of disabled people persists within the sector, and it is yet to be seen how the introduction of disability statements, and the increased strategic role of the funding councils will affect this.

A disabled student from 1985 would hardly recognize the higher education environment now, for so much has changed, and so much of it for the better. But there are no grounds for complacency; the challenges that face the sector in the next decade are no less important than those it has faced in the past. Organizations like Skill, and others who are concerned to see provision for disabled students improve, will need to continue their work if the needs, the rights and the voices of disabled students are to be given the recognition they deserve in the higher education system of the future.

REFERENCES

DES (1978) *Special Educational Needs: Report of a Committee of Enquiry into the Education of Handicapped Children and Young People* (the Warnock Report). London: HMSO.

National Bureau for Handicapped Students (1974) *Proceedings of the Inaugural Meeting 22 November.* London: NBHS (now Skill: National Bureau for Students with Disabilities, 336 Brixton Road, London, SW9 7AA).

Stowell, R. (1987) *Catching Up?* London: NBHS.

11

Sharing skills: international perspectives on policy and practice

Jenny Corbett

INTRODUCTION

This final chapter explores the ways in which we can all learn and share skills within an international network. Through examining different approaches and contexts, the focus will return to the British experience and the ways in which we can adapt for future needs.

The following questions will be raised through an analysis of international approaches:

- What skills are required to support learners in HE?
- Which teaching and learning methods can be generalized?
- Which approaches are specifically related to culture and context?
- How is the concept of 'disability' variously defined in HE?
- What policy appears to be most effective in ensuring entitlement to appropriate services?
- Are there implications for the status of teaching as a skill in HE?
- Why is this initiative largely confined to the new universities?

This sequence of issues to be explored will lead from practice to policy to future directions and planning.

In July, 1995, I attended an international conference organized by the University of New Orleans and held in Innsbruck, Austria. It was titled, 'Tools for Tomorrow: Exchanging International Perspectives on Higher Education and Disability' and provided a stimulating forum for debate. Delegates from the USA, Canada, Britain, Germany, Austria, Italy, Eastern Europe and Australia were able to exchange views on provision for disabled students in higher education. Many were practitioners with direct responsibility for the day-to-day support and guidance of disabled students and staff. The emphasis throughout was upon teaching skills, policy and practice. It offered a more practical approach than is commonly found at academic conferences.

The material in this chapter has been drawn extensively from that conference. To supplement the practical flavour, however, also included are more theoretical references which contextualize these developments within a wider conceptual arena. Through this fusion of the practical and theoretical, at the end of the chapter comes suggestions on future possibilities. They include both the pragmatic, as befits a practical emphasis, and the visionary, offering potential directions for higher education in the twenty-first century.

SHARING SKILLS

Specific skills have been shared in recent initiatives; some are clearly of general value and able to be universally applied while others are of so culturally related a nature that they lose meaning when dislocated from their context. What has emerged within the learning support debate highlights the recent emphasis in HE upon the quality of the teaching and learning experience. Gibbs (1995) goes so far as to suggest that promotion in the university sector may be increasingly linked to teaching excellence. This is an interesting reflection in relation to the learning support services. While much of the most innovative and student-centred teaching materials have arisen from those concerned with improving study skills, this has not been perceived as a potential research area or as the natural location of quality indicators in HE. A genuine commitment to teaching skills in this sector can, therefore, only be demonstrated through a valued status being accorded to the learning support structures.

One of the key facets of effective sharing of skills is that this requires more than an interested management or industrious individuals. It is about systems. As Cain (1995, p.2) recognized:

> Let's be honest. A vice-chancellor pointing to the ramp and declaring that this is progress, or a lone member of staff in student welfare furiously juggling too much work and too little time, until they themselves are disabled by stress, is not full commitment. My experience has taught me that people at the sharp end of things, those at the doing end of things, often know exactly what needs to be done and usually have a good idea of how best to do it. At the risk of sounding like a gardener and not a disabilities advisor, grass roots work needs nurturing and supporting, needs encouragement and a frame to grow up against. Without this framework, this total

approach, change or progress is ultimately hampered and good ideas, or young ideas, never flower and never come to fruition.

The 'total approach' offered by an effective framework or system is graphically illustrated in many of the American universities, where teaching and learning skills form an integral part of an overall policy on quality student services.

At East Stroudsburg University in Pennsylvania, for example, the Learning Skills Co-ordinator offers a comprehensive range of services to help students to become independent learners. These include: reviewing documentation; discussing accommodation; arranging for assessment modifications; classroom adaptations; a reduced course load; additional tutoring; use of drop-in labs; proof-reading assistance; and priority registration. Each semester, the Learning Support Counsellor presents a workshop to peer and professional tutors.

The attention now given to the assessment procedures for students with learning disabilities at American universities is extensive, including the use of computer-based testing (Bennett, 1995) and the more traditional handwritten tests (Nelson, 1995). For students with acknowledged learning disabilities, there are detailed manuals available to guide them through essay writing, note-taking and memory retention strategies (Miller, 1995). Staff handbooks on teaching students with a wide range of disabilities appear to be widely used now in many countries, including Canada, where teaching and learning needs are closely linked to issues of equity (SIAST, 1995).

Much of the skill sharing has general application. Clear communication to staff and students, which shows what is available, where to locate help, and the strategies for securing individual requirements, is beneficial in any context. Availability of teaching materials, guidelines and resources is also generally of value. Above all, the establishment of a system within any higher education institution which supports, sustains and plans for the development of support services is central to the healthy and confident growth of provision.

Where significant differences arise is in the structures of what constitutes a university and in the definitions of disability. It is undeniably true that the widely diverse university sector in the USA, for example, is very different from the traditional university sector more usually found in central Europe. Britain is in an interesting position at present. The new universities may be seen to be emulating much which is part of a system of equity in American higher education, while the old universities are within the European tradition in their student profiles. Within these various conceptions of what constitutes a 'university', there are distinctly contrasting definitions of what 'disability' means in the context of higher education.

DEFINING 'DISABILITY' IN HE

Two aspects of defining disability in higher education present marked contrasts within an international forum. The first is in relation to 'learning disabilities'. The second is in perceptions of what constitutes 'disability' among university students.

Within the UK, the prevalence of students defining themselves as 'dyslexic' has increased significantly over recent years, as earlier chapters in this book testify. A degree of discomfort with so specific a definition of 'learning disability' has been voiced by some learning support teachers in schools, according to a Scottish survey (Duffield *et al.*, 1995). They imply that social and economic factors can influence the learning process to a significant extent and that so narrow a definition is not always helpful.

It is interesting, in the light of these expressed reservations, than American definitions of 'learning disability' are much broader than those used in the British HE system.

Among the 'types of learning disabilities' found in post-secondary students at a Texan college, Rapp (1995) lists the following: abstract reasoning, arithmetic deficit, auditory processing, constructional dyspraxia, dyslexia, language comprehension, long-term memory deficit, long-term retrieval, processing speed, reading deficit, reasoning deficit, short-term memory deficit, spatial organization, spelling dyspraxia, visual processing, writing deficit.

Cynics might suggest that this is a very elaborate and pretentious way of indicating that there are general problems with learning basic skills, especially when the list included 'dyscalculia' (problems with maths) and 'dysgraphia' (problems with hand-writing). Other elements of American definitions, however, are distinctly sinister rather than mildly amusing. Several of the American university presentations at the Innsbruck International Conference (Rapp, 1995; Pearson, 1995) spoke of 'attention deficit' and 'hyperactivity' as recognized learning disabilities which could be treated with medication. The borderline between personality control and learning support is delicate, when drug-taking can be routinely attached to individual learning programmes in HE.

One of the key issues raised by international definitions of what constitutes 'disability' in the university sector is that higher education means something different in different contexts. In America, it is evident that post-secondary students are entering a wide range of institutions, from the most prestigious and highly competitive university 'Ivy League' to a diverse choice of colleges which combine elements of further and higher education. Students with 'learning disabilities' constitute over half of their disabled student population, selecting, as they can, from a wealth of well-supported courses.

In central Europe, this appears not to be the case. While only a limited range of European universities were represented at the international conference, those presenting papers were predominantly concerned with the needs of students who had physical or sensory disabilities. The organization 'Handicap and Studie' located in Utrecht, serves the needs of students with 'physical and mental disabilities'; universities in Bratislava, Linz, Narbonne and Wien all focus upon the specific needs of blind students. This emphasis may reflect a more narrowly academic European tradition of university education, in contrast to the focus upon equity and entitlement which is part of the American rhetoric.

A POLICY FOR ENTITLEMENT

The British university sector can learn much from its American counterpart in relation to designing policy frameworks which really support concepts of equality and entitlement.

While the British Higher Education Quality Council (HEQC, 1995) refers to 'a learner-centred experience' which sets out learner entitlements and responsibilities alongside institutional responsibilities, the July 1995 interim report of the Further and Higher Education Review Programme of the Disability Discrimination Bill states that: 'The HE Charter has no status in law and does not prescribe' (p.29). In this characteristically British manner, it is left to the discretion of individual institutions to decide how they should interpret the anti-discrimination policy. No such options are part of the American approach. Students are told what their rights and responsibilities are, under the Americans with Disabilities Act. Their interests are supported by university staff. In a Canadian example, this support comes from an 'Education Equity Co-ordinator' (Kesler, 1995).

In both America and Canada, student empowerment and assertiveness training courses are provided to help disabled students to address their rights and acknowledge their responsibilities (Birdwell, 1995; Roberts, 1995; Swoboda, 1995). The value of 'mainstreaming' disabled students within the American university sector is noted by observers from other countries, as one Japanese blind woman remarked: 'In Japan, people with disabilities are isolated. We are struggling to be in the mainstream ... Ninety per cent of blind people are trained to do acupuncture or massage. (Naoko Yoshino, quoted in *Visions*, 1995, p.9).

Not only does this policy for entitlement apply to mainstreaming within the university system but it extends to student exchanges in other countries. Disabled students have been significantly under-represented in exchanges abroad, on practical and pragmatic grounds. Now there is a considerable impetus from America and the UK to extend their opportunities for travel to include Central Europe and beyond. The significance for both the personal value of this empowerment and as a model to other disabled students is illustrated by recent research (Matthews, Hameister and Skolnick, 1995; Adams, 1995). It sets disabled students alongside their more adventurous peers as being open to new influences, ready to take risks and able to express themselves as individuals. In itself, this opportunity to travel abroad as a learner is an effective way of breaking the barriers of stereotype.

THE ROLE OF NEW UNIVERSITIES

This concluding section explores both the pragmatic and the visionary aspects of a learning support perspective within international higher education. It is not possible to isolate 'learning support' from what is happening in the rest of the higher education sector generally nor would it be appropriate to do so; the philosophy of supporting new learners into the experience of higher education is integral to the new universities and their missions. The University of East London, for example, states in its 1995–96 Student Handbook mission statement that it is committed 'to widen access further for mature, non-traditionally qualified and ethnic minority students' and 'to provide flexible and responsive study patterns and modes of learning'.

Looking first at the implications of encouraging 'non-traditionally qualified' learners into HE, before exploring the potential of more 'flexible and responsive study patterns', we can view both aspects through pragmatic and visionary lenses.

In Britain, there has recently been considerable disquiet expressed about the inclusion of 'non-traditionally qualified' learners in HE. Daley (1995), Scott-Clark and Rayment (1995) have referred to a fall in standards, a problem in gaining employment after graduation and, the greatest insult, have implied that some universities offer 'dummy degrees'. Smithers, a highly influential British Education professor, has stated: 'We are no longer sure what our higher education system is for' (Smithers, 1995, p.13). He goes on to criticize the former polytechnic sector for having become responsible for what he terms 'pseudo-vocationalism, false disciplines, sets of modules about nothing in particular' (ibid.). While his position may be interpreted as a characteristically right-wing response to innovations, his reservations reflect those expressed by Pat Ainley and myself, coming from an entirely different position. In our paper (Ainley and Corbett, 1994) we were re-addressing Cohen's (1985) critique of the 'new vocationalism' within the context of developments in higher education. We noted that disconnected social skills were being taught in isolation from their cultural context. Within the debate on 'dummy degrees' it is predominant non-traditional, working class, black and disabled students who are the losers in the job market.

When Ainley reflected that 'education without jobs in the 1990s is in the process of replacing the training without jobs of the 1970s and 1980s' (Ainley, 1994, p.28), he was accurately forecasting the present dilemma.

To set against the practical issue of flooding a fragile employment market with devalued graduates, there are the real benefits of increasing the educational experiences of a wider section of the population. This has advantages on a purely intellectual level, creating what Ainley (1994, p.180) calls 'polyconceptualists': students who have vision and insight. He suggests that 'the "demands" of industry have to be set in a wider framework of human cultural and environmental need'. The Department of Employment, however, maintains as its vision for the future an integration of work-based learning into higher education to widen access and make the learning more relevant to the needs of employers (Walker, 1995). In relation to disabled learners, the increased use of new technology is seen as potentially useful in assessment and training, and a vision is required to set standards of user acceptability (TIDE, 1995). Opening up higher education to new learners inevitably brings about changes in practice.

What Smithers (1995) derides as 'set of modules about nothing in particular' has to be seen in the context of new ways of seeing higher education. His is essentially a traditional perspective. There are other ways of looking at what a higher education experience can mean. Gibbs (1995) is a prominent advocate of the importance of teaching skills in higher education. He recognizes that it tends

to be the new universities in Britain which offer the best examples
of the scholarship of teaching. The centrality of the teaching practices to the quality of the student's learning experience is
reinforced by Gibson (1995, p.3), whose reflections on her own
university life as a deaf learner are interesting. She says:

> From my own experience, many eminent and respected academics
> can become their own worst enemies when delivering lectures. The
> way in which they have been allowed to teach over the years may
> neither have changed nor have been challenged, and indeed when
> confronted with a profoundly deaf student who simply asks for the
> lecturer to, for example, stand still, may have a deep psychological
> effect on their wellbeing if such pacing of the classroom floor is
> habitual or this may even create downright hostility.

She accepts that many unconscious patterns of behaviour are hard
to break and that resistance to change is endemic, especially
among teachers who are rarely encouraged to re-evaluate their
practice. Here, teachers in HE can learn from those in the school
sector to reflect on their past practice and re-evaluate this in
response to current needs. If this takes the form of systematic
enquiry, including a theoretical emphasis, it can be both the basis
for ongoing research activity as well as means of improving
performance (Frost, 1995).

Higher education in Britain now includes more non-traditionally
qualified learners than ever before. This has led to a high value
being placed on the quality of teaching, leading to promotion for
excellence of teaching skills (Gosling, 1995). There is also a raised
staff awareness of the support needs of students and an increased
level of co-operation between institutions through the networks of
designated co-ordinators and advisers for students with disabili-
ties/special needs (Brown, 1995). Yet these advantages only apply
to a certain sector of British higher education. There is a huge layer
which remains untouched by this influence and appears uncon-
cerned to change its practice. Herein lies a real danger that a
three-tier HE system may become established, in which the élite
universities from the top tier (the cream which will not be
disturbed), the newer universities from the middle-tier (catering
from a comprehensive mix) and the former polytechnics contain a
disproportionate number of students with evident learning
disabilities (the special education section of HE). This scenario
would be unfortunate, to say the least. It could foster negative
labelling of both students and institutions and reinforce long-held
prejudices. Scott (1995, p.49) encourages us to take a broader
perspective which includes both the tertiary and general further
education colleges as well as the various higher education institu-

tions. He suggests: 'This impression of diversity is heightened if the whole of post-compulsory education is considered.' His emphasis on 'diversity' rather than 'divisiveness' is a valuable avoidance of the cultivation of a categorizing climate in its positive vision of post-compulsory education in the twenty-first century. In reflecting upon Norwegian higher education, Sand, p.20, notes that 'university fundamentalism' can promote stagnation and inertia. Such fundamentalism can be seen to characterize the European higher education tradition. If we are exploring the development of learning support in British HE, we can only do this effectively through an analysis of global economic and political trends.

Marquand and Wright (1995, p.17), in an evaluation of the new British labour movement within Europe, state that, 'The grand narratives of liberalism and socialism no longer carry conviction. Our society is multi-cultural, multi-ethnic, multi-valued ... Elites are suspect; institutions are broken reeds; mistrust is endemic; leadership impossible'. They go on to compare Britain to both America and the rest of Europe and conclude that it has more in common with the European tradition of state power and strong leadership that with the hyper-individualism and cultural disintegration of the US.

Within this tension of competing global influences, will the UK create an HE system which mirrors international differences? Will the old university sector continue to reflect traditional European educational élitism? Will the new universities offer a post-modern approach to cultural disintegration and hyper-individualism? If so, then learning support services and policies for equity become part of this new culture. They reflect the new learning culture of rights rather than privilege. The institutions, for their part, have to become responsive and receptive to change. What is taught and how learners gain their qualifications will no longer be restrained by former expectations. It is an exciting vision, albeit one which calls for re-evaluating how higher education is conceptualized and appraised.

REFERENCES

Adams, M. (1995) Symbolising disability: barriers to European mobility. Paper presented at the second international conference 'Tools for Tomorrow: Exchanging International Perspectives on Higher Education and Disability', Innsbruck.

Ainley, P. (1994) *Degrees of Difference: Higher Education in the 1990s.* London: Lawrence & Wishart.

Ainley, P. and Corbett, J. (1994) From vocationalism to enterprise: social and life skills become personal and transferable. *British Journal of Sociology of Education*, 15(3), 365–74.

Bennett, R. (1995) Computer-based testing for examiners with disabilities: on the road to generalised accommodation. Paper presented at the second international conference, 'Tools for Tomorrow: Exchanging International Perspectives on Higher Education and Disability', Innsbruck.

Birdwell, M. (1995) Empowering students for post-secondary success. Paper presented at the second international conference, 'Tools for Tomorrow: Exchanging International Perspectives on Higher Education and Disability', Innsbruck.

Brown, P. (1995) A degree of change – advances in provision for students with disabilities/special needs in the Scottish Higher Education Sector. *Skill Journal*, **52**, 21–4.

Cain, S. (1995) How We Did It: Developing Practical Solutions for Disabled Students. The University Experience. Paper presented at 'Tools for Tomorrow: Exchanging International Perspectives on Higher Education Disability', Innsbruck.

Cohen, P. (1985) Against the new vocationalism. In I. Bates, J. Clarke, P. Cohen, D. Finn, R. Moore, and P. Willis, (eds) *Schooling for the Dole?: The New Vocationalism*. Basingstoke: Macmillan.

Comenius University, Bratislava (1995) University Study for Visually Impaired Students. Paper presented at the second international conference, 'Tools for Tomorrow: Exchanging International Perspectives on Higher Education and Disability', Innsbruck.

Daley, J. (1995) The fall in A-level standards looks irreversible, so what should we do about education now? *The Times*, 17, August, 14.

Department for Education and Employment (1995) *Further and Higher Education Review Programme: Disability Discrimination Bill. Interim Report, July 1995*. London: DFEE.

Duffield, J., Brown, S. and Riddell, S. (1995), The post-Warnock learning support teacher: Where do specific learning difficulties fit in? *Support for Learning*, **10** (1) 22–8.

European Commission (1995) *Telematics for the Integration of Disabled and Elderly People*. Brussels: EC.

Frost, D. (1995) Integrating systematic enquiry into everyday professional practice: toward some principles of procedure. *British Educational Research Journal*, **21** (3), 307–21.

Gibbs, G. (1995) How can promoting excellent teachers promote excellent teaching? *Innovations in Education and International Training*, **32** (1), 74–84.

Gibson, R. (1995) *Breaking the Sound Barrier*. Paper presented at the second international conference, 'Tools for Tomorrow: Exchanging International Perspectives on Higher Education and Disability', Innsbruck.

Gosling, D. (1995) Staff personal and professional development: policy and strategy framework. *Quality Digest*, **3**, 1–4.

Handicap and Studie (1995) Handicap and Studie: A National Institute Supporting Students with Disabilities. Paper presented at the second international conference, 'Tools for Tomorrow: Exchanging International Perspectives on Higher Education and Disability', Innsbruck.

HEQC (1995) *A Quality Assurance Framework for Guidance and Learner Support in Higher Education*. London: HEQC.

Johannes Keplar University, Linz (1995) Computer Science for the Blind. Paper presented at the second international conference, 'Tools for Tomorrow: Exchanging International Perspectives on Higher Education and Disability, Innsbruck.

Kesler, T. (1995) Jottings from the den of Equity, *Communicator*, 6 (2), 4.

Marquand, D. and Wright, A. (1995) New Labour: the Euro-option, *New Statesman & Society*, 1 September, 16–17.

Matthews, P., Hameister, B. and Skolnick, B. (1995) No barriers to study. Paper presented at the second international conference, 'Tools for Tomorrow: Exchanging International Perspectives on Higher Education and Disability', Innsbruck.

Miller, E. (1995) Instructional Strategies for Students with Learning Disabilities. Paper presented at the second international conference, 'Tools for Tomorrow: Exchanging International Perspectives on Higher Education and Disability', Innsbruck.

Nelson, C. (1995) Paper and pencil testing for candidates with disabilities: determining eligibility and providing accommodations. Paper presented at the second international conference, 'Tools for Tomorrow: Exchanging International Perspectives on Higher Education and Disability', Innsbruck.

Pearson, C. (1995) Assessing and serving students with learning disorders. Paper presented at the second international conference, 'Tools for Tomorrow: Exchanging International Perspectives on Higher Education and Disability', Innsbruck.

Rapp, R. (1995) Accommodations for postsecondary students with learning disabilities: a balancing act. Paper presented at the second international conference, 'Tools for Tomorrow: Exchanging International Perspectives on Higher Education and Disability', Innsbruck.

Roberts, D. (1995) Teaching study skills to students with learning disabilities. Paper presented at the second international conference, 'Tools for Tomorrow: Exchanging International Perspectives on Higher Education and Disability', Innsbruck.

Sand, G. (1994) 'Knowledge is power for a small country.' In *Ten Minutes on the University of Trondheim*. Norway, University of Trondheim.

Scott, P. (1995) *The Meanings of Mass Higher Education*. Buckingham: Society for Research into Higher Education and Open University Press.

Scott-Clark, C. and Rayment, T. (1995) Scandal of our dummy degrees, *The Sunday Times*, 3 September, 12–13.

SIAST (1995) *Teaching Students with Disabilities*. Saskatoon: Saskatchewan Institute of Applied Science and Technology.

Smithers, A. (1995) Students on the road to nowhere, *The Sunday Times*, 3 September, 13.

Swoboda, D. (1995) Learning strategies seminar. Paper presented at the second international conference, 'Tools for Tomorrow: Exchanging

International Perspectives on Higher Education and Disability', Innsbruck.

Trondheim University (1994) *Ten Minutes on the University of Trondheim*, Trondheim: University of Trondheim.

University of San Francisco (1995) *USF Services for the Learning Disabled*. San Francisco: USF.

Vigouroux, N., Seiler, F. and Truillet, P. (1995) Access to electronic documents in higher education for blind students: the smart system on network. Paper presented at the second international conference, 'Tools for Tomorrow: Exchanging International Perspectives on Higher Education and Disability', Innsbruck.

Visions (1995) Opportunities for persons with disabilities in US impress Japanese visitor. *Visions*, **3** (2), 9.

Walker, B. (1995) Higher education: making the skills link, *Insight*, Summer, 11–13.

Name Index

Subject Index